Syllable Savvy Spelling

Syl³ la² ble³

Sav³ vy²

Spel⁴ ling⁴

A simple strategy that spells success.

Karen K. Newell

Learn For Your Life

Third Edition 2015

Cover Design by Christy Short

Learn For Your Life Publishing
Camp Hill, PA 17011

www.Learn4YourLife.com

Instructor's Guide

Welcome to Syllable Savvy Spelling. This simple technique will not only improve your students' spelling scores this year, but will provide them with a successful strategy that will improve their spelling ability for years to come. In fact, you will likely find that your own ability to spell difficult words is improved after teaching this technique.

THREE COLUMN APPROACH

You will notice that each lesson has three columns. The first is the Phonetic Column. This allows the student to sound out the word using the common dictionary symbols for each phonetic sound. The second column displays the word as it is usually written. The third column is the Syllable Column and prints the words in syllables and gives the number of letters in each syllable. This column prompts the student to focus on the syllables in each word, and the specific letters in the syllables.

Phonetic Column

The Phonetic Column gives the dictionary symbols to allow the student to sound out the word. This has two benefits. First, the student can practice the words each day without having the answer right in plain view simply by folding the lesson page so only the first column is showing. As an alternative to folding the paper, another sheet of paper can be placed over the second and third columns. Second, seeing only the phonetic column allows the student to work independently, rather than have a teacher or partner dictate the word without them seeing it.

The symbols used in Syllable Savvy are common symbols used in dictionaries. The exception is the short vowel sound. This is the sound one would hear preceding a "ck" at the end of the word (ie. back, deck, sick, lock, duck). In many dictionaries, the short sound is marked with a curved line, somewhat like a smile, over the letter. In Syllable Savvy, the short vowel sound has no symbol. The long vowel sound is marked with the standard flat line over the vowel. (ie, bāke, mē, līke, hōpe, tūne)

At the bottom of each lesson page, is a quick pronunciation key which lists the sounds indicated by the different marks. Apart from the short and long vowel sounds, it is not necessary for the student to attempt to memorize any of the other marks. Of course, they will get much more familiar with these marks by using Syllable Savvy Spelling.

One other sound should be mentioned, which is the schwa sound, indicated by the symbol which looks like an upside down e. This is the vowel sound in the non-stressed syllables which rhymes with "duh." It may be spelled with an "a", "e", "i", o," u", or "y".

The pronunciation marks provided are based on one common pronunciation for the word. Some words have different pronunciations, many of which are regional. If the pronunciation listed is different than that used in your home, you have three options. One, the word on the lesson may be erased with white out, and the familiar pronunciation substituted. Or, the more familiar pronunciation can be written above the one on the lesson page, emphasizing to the students that there is more than one correct way to pronounce a word. Finally, one can acknowledge the differences with the student and leave the word as it is. Probably, it is best to use whatever approach is preferred by the student.

Spelling texts for fifth grade and above

also have the stressed syllables underlined. It should be noted that some words represent more than one part of speech and the pronunciation may be different. For instance, "content" as a noun has the first syllable stressed. "Content" as an adjective as the second syllable stressed. Most of the time we have used the pronunciation for the noun form since it is generally more common.

PHONETIC COLUMN:
A WARNING

It should be noted that some younger children in lower grades may have difficulty with the Phonetic Column. It may be confusing to some students when they are presented with the "wrong" letters and the phonetic marks may reinforce using the wrong letters. Of course, the purpose of Syllable Savvy is to promote correct spelling, and if a student finds the phonetic "clues" confusing, this is counter-productive. However, other aspects of Syllable Savvy can still be used. If you determine the phonetic marks are confusing to your student, you may choose not to emphasize the Phonetic Column. In several more months, or even a year, the student may be ready to sound out the word from the phonetic spelling.

If you chose not to use the Phonetic Column for a younger child, there are a few techniques that could be employed to keep the benefit of the phonetic clues. First, a picture or sample sentence can be written on one side of an index card, and the other two columns written on the opposite side. For instance, if the spelling word is "ocean", the first side could have the sentence, "Let's go swim in the o......" and have the waves of the sea drawn on the card. The opposite side of the card could list the regular spelling and the Syllable Column.

Another technique to allow the student to work independently on their spelling list without seeing the word each time they practice it; is to record the word and a sentence using the word with a tape player or computer. The student can listen to hear the spoken word and then write the word on paper.

Of course, the old fashioned way of having a parent or partner read the words on the list to the student can still be used. One of the values of Syllable Savvy Spelling is that it allows the student to study all of the words independently. Some younger students, however, are not necessarily ready for that independence and do better working with someone else.

Middle Column

The middle column displays the word with its standard spelling. This is the way the students will encounter the word and in most cases they will be familiar with it. It is obvious that it is much easier to read a familiar word than it is to spell it.

Syllable Column

The Syllable Column breaks each word into its syllables. This is the natural way to write complex words. It also has the advantage of giving the students syllables that are usually only two to four letters long. That is much less intimidating than facing a long word with what appears to be an unattainable number of letters.

After each syllable, the number of letters in that syllable is displayed in superscript. This helps the student to focus on the specific letters in each syllable.

The number at the end of the syllable also aids the students in correcting their own work. Often students will look at a longer word they have just written and think it looks "about right" and not compare each letter on their list and the master list. Day after day, this reinforces writing the word incorrectly. By writing the word in syllables, then recording how many letters they correctly wrote in each syllable, the student receives immediate feedback. It also becomes more obvious to them if one letter is incorrect.

FIVE EXTRA SPACES

Each lesson consists of 20 words. However, only 15 words are listed on the Lesson Page. This is because it is important to include in the students' study of spelling those words that are particularly important for them. These words can include words they misspelled from previous spelling lessons, words they misspell in their creative writing, or words that are part of their science, social studies, or other unit studies.

ONE LESSON PER WEEK

Each Syllable Savvy Spelling level consists of thirty weekly lessons. Each lesson consists of four pages. The fifth day of the week is the spelling test.

You will notice that each lesson is printed two times with two sets of blank lines on the opposing pages. This is so the students have the Phonetic Column in front of them as they do their exercises. They will use the first page for Days 1 and 2, then turn to the second page for Days 3 and 4.

HOW IT WORKS

1st Day

The first day of the lesson, the student will first encounter the new spelling words. This is most effective if it is done one-on-one with the instructor. After the first day, the student will practice the words independently. Of course, some older students prefer to work independently, and once they have been taught the steps below, they may prefer to do even the first day's work on their own.

1. Look at the spelling word in the middle column. For most of the words in this program, the word will be familiar to the students. Read the word together.
2. Look at the pronunciation of the word in the first column or Phonetic Column. Help the student sound the word out using the pronunciation key at the bottom of the page.
3. Look at each syllable in the Syllable Column. Ask, "Is this the way you would expect this syllable to be written? Is there anything tricky or difficult here?" Thankfully, most syllables aren't too difficult.
4. Any letters that are not expected can be underlined with a colored pencil. This is an optional step; but some students find that the focus required to identify the unexpected letters helps to cement them in their memory.
5. Cover the middle and third columns so they are not visible. Then the student will write the word on the correct line on the opposing page. They should write it in syllables with breaks between each syllable.
6. After the entire word is written, the student will look at the Syllable Column again to correct the word. The student checks the number of letters in each syllable as recorded in the Syllable Column with the letters they actually wrote on their page. If the letters are all correct, the student moves to the next syllable.
7. Syllable by syllable the student checks

the letters they have written with the word on the Syllable Column.

8. If all syllables in the word were written correctly, color in the box at the end of the line. That gives a small but tangible pat ont he back for their good work.
9. Next move to the next word on the spelling list.
10. If any part of the word was missed, it needs to be written again on a separate sheet of paper. Focus specific attention on the syllable(s) missed.
11. Any missed letters can be underlined on the Syllable Column of the lesson. This will flag the student to note those letters while doing their daily review.

HOW IT WORKS
2nd - 4th Days

On the second, third, and fourth days of the week, the student will practice writing their words using the same technique. Even if they worked with the teacher the first day, they will do these practice sessions alone.

Students begin by reviewing the first page of the lesson. Any unusual spellings or difficult words have been marked on this page previously.

Then students will either fold the page to show only the Phonetic Column, or cover the second two columns with another sheet of the paper. They then proceed to write the words in the column marked for that day. Words are written syllable by syllable as before.

Before proceeding to the next word, students self-correct the word they just wrote. They verify every letter in every syllable. At the end of each syllable, they write the number of correct letters. If all letters in a word are correct, they indicate the word was written correctly by coloring in the box.

Incorrect words must be rewritten on a separate page. They need to write each word until every syllable is written correctly

ALTERNATIVE

As an alternative to writing in the book, a student can fold a regular piece of lined writing paper in half the long way. That makes two columns on each side, or four total for the front and back. They can use the same paper for one week. They can cover the second and third columns with their writing paper as they proceed down the page.

SPELLING TEST
5th Day

The last day of the week, the spelling test is given. The teacher dictates each word and the student writes it on a separate sheet of paper.

GRADING

Usually, with a twenty word spelling list, each word is worth five points. Therefore, the grade to the test can be determined by multiplying the number of incorrect words on the test by five, and subtracting the product from 100 percent.

The daily practices can be graded and counted as quiz grades for students who need additional help in spelling. On a quiz, each syllable can be counted as two points. Therefore, a student is getting partial credit for the syllables they write correctly. The words written on the first day are not included as a quiz grade, as the student is encountering the word for the first time. The three quiz grades can be averaged. The quiz grades can be equal to one test grade.

An alternative method is to give one bonus point for each daily practice page. This gives credit to the student for keeping on track and making progress through the week.

SPELLING RULES

You will notice that many of the words have tiny chalk boards with a single letter on it. This letter refers to the appropriate rule in the Spelling Rules index in the back of the book.

We have two goals with these Spelling Rules. First, we want to show common rules which will assist student's spelling ability without having them memorize every possible rule in the English language. The point is not to memorize rules, but to group common spelling patterns so they are easier to remember.

Second, an occasional review of the spelling rules will cement the pattern in their mind as well as the correct spelling of words they have learned. You might consider giving a monthly spot quiz to see if they can spell words from one or two rules.

Many students find it helpful to keep a list of words with a common pattern. This is a great technique in teaching phonics in kindergarten through second grade, but can be continued with spelling patterns in older grades as well. Students may like to write the words directly on the Spelling Rules page, or keep a separate notebook.

TEACHING TIPS

It takes discipline for a student to develop the habit of sounding out each syllable phonetically while writing the letters simultaneously. Therefore, it takes effort on your part to coach them in developing that skill. It is an effort well worth your time that will pay off for both of you.

On the first day, as the child is writing the weekly list for the first time, listen that he or she verbalizes each syllable as it is written. If they do not, ask them to rewrite it while speaking it. Occasionally during the week you can also listen and remind them to develop this habit.

Visual learners often find that highlighting the vowels with a yellow highlighter helps them to remember them. Some have found that using a different colored highlighter for different vowel combinations is helpful. However, there are only a few colors of highlighters so this may not be as useful unless you also keep a variety of colored markers on hand as well.

Kinetic learners who like motion or touch can write their words in the air, draw them on a velvet covered board, or spell them in cursive with their toes. Young dancers particularly like that last technique.

Keeping a notebook of common spelling patterns is useful for younger students. However, even older students find it helpful for certain patterns such as "ough" or "sion." As an alternative to a notebook, use the Spelling Rules pages or the extra pages at the end of the book as a place to write hard to remember words. A quick review once a month will enable students to remember words previously learned and connect them to new ones as they are presented.

Day 1

1. ______________________ ☐
2. ______________________ ☐
3. ______________________ ☐
4. ______________________ ☐
5. ______________________ ☐
6. ______________________ ☐
7. ______________________ ☐
8. ______________________ ☐
9. ______________________ ☐
10. ______________________ ☐
11. ______________________ ☐
12. ______________________ ☐
13. ______________________ ☐
14. ______________________ ☐
15. ______________________ ☐
16. ______________________ ☐
17. ______________________ ☐
18. ______________________ ☐
19. ______________________ ☐
20. ______________________ ☐

Day 2

1. ______________________ ☐
2. ______________________ ☐
3. ______________________ ☐
4. ______________________ ☐
5. ______________________ ☐
6. ______________________ ☐
7. ______________________ ☐
8. ______________________ ☐
9. ______________________ ☐
10. ______________________ ☐
11. ______________________ ☐
12. ______________________ ☐
13. ______________________ ☐
14. ______________________ ☐
15. ______________________ ☐
16. ______________________ ☐
17. ______________________ ☐
18. ______________________ ☐
19. ______________________ ☐
20. ______________________ ☐

ā	âr	är	er	ē	ēr	ī	ō	ŏŏ	ôr	ow	oy	ū	zh	ə
day	air	far	her	bee	tear	light	rope	book	for	cow	boy	tune	vision	item

Lesson 1

1.	mont gum er ē	Montgomery	Mont^{4} gom^{3} er^{2} y^{1}
2.	al ə bam ə	Alabama	Al^{2} a^{1} bam^{3} a^{1}
3.	jan yū âr ē	January	Jan^{3} u^{1} ar^{2} y^{1}
4.	feb rū âr ē*	February	Feb^{3} ru^{2} ar^{2} y^{1}
5.	märch	March	March^{5}
6.	ā prəl	April	A^{1} pril^{4}
7.	mā	May	May^{3}
8.	jūn	June	June^{4}
9.	jə lī	July	Ju^{2} ly^{2}
10.	o gəst	August	Au^{2} gust^{4}
11.	sep tem ber	September	Sep^{3} tem^{3} ber^{3}
12.	ok tō ber	October	Oc^{2} to^{2} ber^{3}
13.	nō vem ber	November	No^{2} vem^{3} ber^{3}
14.	dē sem ber	December	De^{2} cem^{3} ber^{3}
15.	munth lē	monthly	month^{5} ly^{2}
16.			
17.			
18.			
19.			
20.			

G

*Read the G Rule. These words have a recommended "spelling pronunciations" due to unusual spellings.

ā	âr	är	er	ē	ēr	ī	ō	ŏŏ	ôr	ow	oy	ū	zh	ə
day	air	far	her	bee	tear	light	rope	book	for	cow	boy	tune	vision	item

Day 3

1. ______________________ ☐
2. ______________________ ☐
3. ______________________ ☐
4. ______________________ ☐
5. ______________________ ☐
6. ______________________ ☐
7. ______________________ ☐
8. ______________________ ☐
9. ______________________ ☐
10. ______________________ ☐
11. ______________________ ☐
12. ______________________ ☐
13. ______________________ ☐
14. ______________________ ☐
15. ______________________ ☐
16. ______________________ ☐
17. ______________________ ☐
18. ______________________ ☐
19. ______________________ ☐
20. ______________________ ☐

Day 4

1. ______________________ ☐
2. ______________________ ☐
3. ______________________ ☐
4. ______________________ ☐
5. ______________________ ☐
6. ______________________ ☐
7. ______________________ ☐
8. ______________________ ☐
9. ______________________ ☐
10. ______________________ ☐
11. ______________________ ☐
12. ______________________ ☐
13. ______________________ ☐
14. ______________________ ☐
15. ______________________ ☐
16. ______________________ ☐
17. ______________________ ☐
18. ______________________ ☐
19. ______________________ ☐
20. ______________________ ☐

ā	âr	är	er	ē	ēr	ī	ō	ŏŏ	ôr	ow	oy	ū	zh	ə
day	air	far	her	bee	tear	light	rope	book	for	cow	boy	tune	vision	item

Lesson 1b

1.	mont gum er ē	Montgomery	Mont^4 gom^3 er^2 y^1
2.	al ə bam ə	Alabama	Al^2 a^1 bam^3 a^1
3.	jan yū âr ē	January	Jan^3 u^1 ar^2 y^1
4.	feb rū âr ē*	February	Feb^3 ru^2 ar^2 y^1
5.	märch	March	March^5
6.	ā prəl	April	A^1 pril^4
7.	mā	May	May^3
8.	jūn	June	June^4
9.	jə lī	July	Ju^2 ly^2
10.	o gəst	August	Au^2 gust^4
11.	sep tem ber	September	Sep^3 tem^3 ber^3
12.	ok tō ber	October	Oc^2 to^2 ber^3
13.	nō vem ber	November	No^2 vem^3 ber^3
14.	dē sem ber	December	De^2 cem^3 ber^3
15.	munth lē	monthly	month^5 ly^2
16.			
17.			
18.			
19.			
20.			

ā	âr	är	er	ē	ēr	ī	ō	ŏŏ	ôr	ow	oy	ū	zh	ə
day	air	far	her	bee	tear	light	rope	book	for	cow	boy	tune	vision	item

Day 1

1. ____________________ ☐
2. ____________________ ☐
3. ____________________ ☐
4. ____________________ ☐
5. ____________________ ☐
6. ____________________ ☐
7. ____________________ ☐
8. ____________________ ☐
9. ____________________ ☐
10. ____________________ ☐
11. ____________________ ☐
12. ____________________ ☐
13. ____________________ ☐
14. ____________________ ☐
15. ____________________ ☐
16. ____________________ ☐
17. ____________________ ☐
18. ____________________ ☐
19. ____________________ ☐
20. ____________________ ☐

Day 2

1. ____________________ ☐
2. ____________________ ☐
3. ____________________ ☐
4. ____________________ ☐
5. ____________________ ☐
6. ____________________ ☐
7. ____________________ ☐
8. ____________________ ☐
9. ____________________ ☐
10. ____________________ ☐
11. ____________________ ☐
12. ____________________ ☐
13. ____________________ ☐
14. ____________________ ☐
15. ____________________ ☐
16. ____________________ ☐
17. ____________________ ☐
18. ____________________ ☐
19. ____________________ ☐
20. ____________________ ☐

ā	**âr**	**är**	**er**	**ē**	**ēr**	**ī**	**ō**	**ŏŏ**	**ôr**	**ow**	**oy**	**ū**	**zh**	**ə**
day	air	far	her	bee	tear	light	rope	book	for	cow	boy	tune	vision	item

Lesson 2

1.	**jū nō**	**Juneau**	**Ju^{2} neau^{4}**	
2.	**ə las kə**	**Alaska**	**A^{1} las^{3} ka^{2}**	
3.	**bē kuz**	**because**	**be^{2} cause^{5}**	
4.	**eks ept**	**except**	**ex^{2} cept^{4}**	
5.	**plēz**	**please**	**please^{6}**	
6.	**vyū**	**view**	**view^{4}**	S
7.	**hīt**	**height**	**height^{6}**	S
8.	**strāt**	**straight**	**straight^{8}**	
9.	**ān ker**	**anchor**	**an^{2} chor^{4}**	Q
10.	**dis pens**	**dispense**	**dis^{3} pense^{5}**	
11.	**mown tən**	**mountain**	**moun^{4} tain^{4}**	
12.	**fown tən**	**fountain**	**foun^{4} tain^{4}**	
13.	**sowr**	**sour**	**sour^{4}**	
14.	**dī ə gram**	**diagram**	**di^{2} a^{1} gram^{4}**	
15.	**top ik**	**topic**	**top^{3} ic^{2}**	
16.				
17.				
18.				
19.				
20.				

ā	**âr**	**är**	**er**	**ē**	**ēr**	**ī**	**ō**	**ŏŏ**	**ôr**	**ow**	**oy**	**ū**	**zh**	**ə**
day	air	far	her	bee	tear	light	rope	book	for	cow	boy	tune	vision	item

Syllable Savvy Spelling Four

Day 3		Day 4	
1.	☐	1.	☐
2.	☐	2.	☐
3.	☐	3.	☐
4.	☐	4.	☐
5.	☐	5.	☐
6.	☐	6.	☐
7.	☐	7.	☐
8.	☐	8.	☐
9.	☐	9.	☐
10.	☐	10.	☐
11.	☐	11.	☐
12.	☐	12.	☐
13.	☐	13.	☐
14.	☐	14.	☐
15.	☐	15.	☐
16.	☐	16.	☐
17.	☐	17.	☐
18.	☐	18.	☐
19.	☐	19.	☐
20.	☐	20.	☐

ā	âr	är	er	ē	ēr	ī	ō	ŏŏ	ôr	ow	oy	ū	zh	ə
day	air	far	her	bee	tear	light	rope	book	for	cow	boy	tune	vision	item

Lesson 2b

1.	jū nō	Juneau	Ju^{2} neau^{4}
2.	ə las kə	Alaska	A^{1} las^{3} ka^{2}
3.	bē kuz	because	be^{2} cause^{5}
4.	eks ept	except	ex^{2} cept^{4}
5.	plēz	please	please^{6}
6.	vyū	view	view^{4}
7.	hīt	height	height^{6}
8.	strāt	straight	straight^{8}
9.	ān ker	anchor	an^{2} chor^{4}
10.	dis pens	dispense	dis^{3} pense^{5}
11.	mown tən	mountain	moun^{4} tain^{4}
12.	fown tən	fountain	foun^{4} tain^{4}
13.	sowr	sour	sour^{4}
14.	dī ə gram	diagram	di^{2} a^{1} gram^{4}
15.	top ik	topic	top^{3} ic^{2}
16.			
17.			
18.			
19.			
20.			

ā	âr	är	er	ē	ēr	ī	ō	ŏŏ	ôr	ow	oy	ū	zh	ə
day	air	far	her	bee	tear	light	rope	book	for	cow	boy	tune	vision	item

Day 1

1. ______________________ ☐
2. ______________________ ☐
3. ______________________ ☐
4. ______________________ ☐
5. ______________________ ☐
6. ______________________ ☐
7. ______________________ ☐
8. ______________________ ☐
9. ______________________ ☐
10. ______________________ ☐
11. ______________________ ☐
12. ______________________ ☐
13. ______________________ ☐
14. ______________________ ☐
15. ______________________ ☐
16. ______________________ ☐
17. ______________________ ☐
18. ______________________ ☐
19. ______________________ ☐
20. ______________________ ☐

Day 2

1. ______________________ ☐
2. ______________________ ☐
3. ______________________ ☐
4. ______________________ ☐
5. ______________________ ☐
6. ______________________ ☐
7. ______________________ ☐
8. ______________________ ☐
9. ______________________ ☐
10. ______________________ ☐
11. ______________________ ☐
12. ______________________ ☐
13. ______________________ ☐
14. ______________________ ☐
15. ______________________ ☐
16. ______________________ ☐
17. ______________________ ☐
18. ______________________ ☐
19. ______________________ ☐
20. ______________________ ☐

ā	âr	är	er	ē	ēr	ī	ō	ŏŏ	ôr	ow	oy	ū	zh	ə
day	air	far	her	bee	tear	light	rope	book	for	cow	boy	tune	vision	item

Lesson 3

1.	fē niks	Phoenix	Phoe[4] nix[3]
2.	âr i zō nə	Arizona	Ar[2] i[1] zo[2] na[2]
3.	o kwə	aqua	a[1] qua[3]
4.	lav en der	lavender	lav[3] en[2] der[3]
5.	bāj	beige	beige[5]
6.	ter koyz	turquoise	tur[3] quoise[6]
7.	pēch	peach	peach[5]
8.	tēl	teal	teal[4]
9.	mə rūn	maroon	ma[2] roon[4]
10.	ber gən dē	burgundy	bur[3] gun[3] dy[2]
11.	roy əl	royal	roy[3] al[2]
12.	skär lit	scarlet	scar[4] let[3]
13.	e bən ē	ebony	eb[2] o[1] ny[2]
14.	sa mən	salmon	sal[3] mon[3]
15.	fyū shwo	fuchsia	fu[2] chsia[5]
16.			
17.			
18.			
19.			
20.			

ā	âr	är	er	ē	ēr	ī	ō	ŏŏ	ôr	ow	oy	ū	zh	ə
day	air	far	her	bee	tear	light	rope	book	for	cow	boy	tune	vision	item

Day 3

1. ______________________ ☐
2. ______________________ ☐
3. ______________________ ☐
4. ______________________ ☐
5. ______________________ ☐
6. ______________________ ☐
7. ______________________ ☐
8. ______________________ ☐
9. ______________________ ☐
10. ______________________ ☐
11. ______________________ ☐
12. ______________________ ☐
13. ______________________ ☐
14. ______________________ ☐
15. ______________________ ☐
16. ______________________ ☐
17. ______________________ ☐
18. ______________________ ☐
19. ______________________ ☐
20. ______________________ ☐

Day 4

1. ______________________ ☐
2. ______________________ ☐
3. ______________________ ☐
4. ______________________ ☐
5. ______________________ ☐
6. ______________________ ☐
7. ______________________ ☐
8. ______________________ ☐
9. ______________________ ☐
10. ______________________ ☐
11. ______________________ ☐
12. ______________________ ☐
13. ______________________ ☐
14. ______________________ ☐
15. ______________________ ☐
16. ______________________ ☐
17. ______________________ ☐
18. ______________________ ☐
19. ______________________ ☐
20. ______________________ ☐

ā	âr	är	er	ē	ēr	ī	ō	ŏŏ	ôr	ow	oy	ū	zh	ə
day	air	far	her	bee	tear	light	rope	book	for	cow	boy	tune	vision	item

Lesson 3b

1.	fē niks	Phoenix	Phoe^{4} nix^{3}
2.	âr i zō nə	Arizona	Ar^{2} i^{1} zo^{2} na^{2}
3.	o kwə	aqua	a^{1} qua^{3}
4.	lav en der	lavender	lav^{3} en^{2} der^{3}
5.	bāj	beige	beige^{5}
6.	ter koyz	turquoise	tur^{3} quoise^{6}
7.	pēch	peach	peach^{5}
8.	tēl	teal	teal^{4}
9.	mə rūn	maroon	ma^{2} roon^{4}
10.	ber gən dē	burgundy	bur^{3} gun^{3} dy^{2}
11.	roy əl	royal	roy^{3} al^{2}
12.	skär lit	scarlet	scar^{4} let^{3}
13.	e bən ē	ebony	eb^{2} o^{1} ny^{2}
14.	sa mən	salmon	sal^{3} mon^{3}
15.	fyū shwo	fuchsia	fu^{2} chsia^{5}
16.			
17.			
18.			
19.			
20.			

ā	âr	är	er	ē	ēr	ī	ō	ŏŏ	ôr	ow	oy	ū	zh	ə
day	air	far	her	bee	tear	light	rope	book	for	cow	boy	tune	vision	item

Day 1		Day 2	
1.	☐	1.	☐
2.	☐	2.	☐
3.	☐	3.	☐
4.	☐	4.	☐
5.	☐	5.	☐
6.	☐	6.	☐
7.	☐	7.	☐
8.	☐	8.	☐
9.	☐	9.	☐
10.	☐	10.	☐
11.	☐	11.	☐
12.	☐	12.	☐
13.	☐	13.	☐
14.	☐	14.	☐
15.	☐	15.	☐
16.	☐	16.	☐
17.	☐	17.	☐
18.	☐	18.	☐
19.	☐	19.	☐
20.	☐	20.	☐

ā	**âr**	**är**	**er**	**ē**	**ēr**	**ī**	**ō**	**ŏŏ**	**ôr**	**ow**	**oy**	**ū**	**zh**	**ə**
day	air	far	her	bee	tear	light	rope	book	for	cow	boy	tune	vision	item

Lesson 4

1.	li dl rok	Little Rock	Lit^{3} tle^{3} Rock^{4}	
2.	är kan sə	Arkansas	Ar^{2} kan^{3} sas^{3}	
3.	jū ish	Jewish	Jew^{3} ish^{3}	
4.	sin ə gog	synagogue	syn^{3} a^{1} gogue^{5}	
5.	krīst	Christ	Christ^{6}	
6.	kris məs	Christmas	Christ^{6} mas^{3}	
7.	kris chən	Christian	Chris^{5} tian^{4}	T
8.	muz lim	Muslim	Mus^{3} lim^{3}	
9.	iz lom	Islam	Is^{2} lam^{3}	
10.	ī dēl	ideal	i^{1} deal^{4}	
11.	prō vīd	provide	pro^{3} vide^{4}	
12.	prō vī zhn	provision	pro^{3} vi^{2} sion^{4}	T
13.	kom plex	complex	com^{3} plex^{4}	
14.	ə long	along	a^{1} long^{4}	
15.	kuv erd	covered	cov^{3} er^{2}ed^{2}	J
16.				
17.				
18.				
19.				
20.				

ā	âr	är	er	ē	ēr	ī	ō	ŏŏ	ôr	ow	oy	ū	zh	ə
day	air	far	her	bee	tear	light	rope	book	for	cow	boy	tune	vision	item

Syllable Savvy Spelling Four

Day 3

1. ______________________ ☐
2. ______________________ ☐
3. ______________________ ☐
4. ______________________ ☐
5. ______________________ ☐
6. ______________________ ☐
7. ______________________ ☐
8. ______________________ ☐
9. ______________________ ☐
10. ______________________ ☐
11. ______________________ ☐
12. ______________________ ☐
13. ______________________ ☐
14. ______________________ ☐
15. ______________________ ☐
16. ______________________ ☐
17. ______________________ ☐
18. ______________________ ☐
19. ______________________ ☐
20. ______________________ ☐

Day 4

1. ______________________ ☐
2. ______________________ ☐
3. ______________________ ☐
4. ______________________ ☐
5. ______________________ ☐
6. ______________________ ☐
7. ______________________ ☐
8. ______________________ ☐
9. ______________________ ☐
10. ______________________ ☐
11. ______________________ ☐
12. ______________________ ☐
13. ______________________ ☐
14. ______________________ ☐
15. ______________________ ☐
16. ______________________ ☐
17. ______________________ ☐
18. ______________________ ☐
19. ______________________ ☐
20. ______________________ ☐

ā	âr	är	er	ē	ēr	ī	ō	ŏŏ	ôr	ow	oy	ū	zh	ə
day	air	far	her	bee	tear	light	rope	book	for	cow	boy	tune	vision	item

Lesson 4b

1.	li dl rok	Little Rock	Lit^{3} tle^{3} Rock^{4}
2.	är kan sə	Arkansas	Ar^{2} kan^{3} sas^{3}
3.	jū ish	Jewish	Jew^{3} ish^{3}
4.	sin ə gog	synagogue	syn^{3} a^{1} gogue^{5}
5.	krīst	Christ	Christ^{6}
6.	kris məs	Christmas	Christ^{6} mas^{3}
7.	kris chən	Christian	Chris^{5} tian^{4}
8.	muz lim	Muslim	Mus^{3} lim^{3}
9.	iz lom	Islam	Is^{2} lam^{3}
10.	ī dēl	ideal	i^{1} deal^{4}
11.	prō vīd	provide	pro^{3} vide^{4}
12.	prō vī zhn	provision	pro^{3} vi^{2} sion^{4}
13.	kom plex	complex	com^{3} plex^{4}
14.	ə long	along	a^{1} long^{4}
15.	kuv erd	covered	cov^{3} er^{2}ed^{2}
16.			
17.			
18.			
19.			
20.			

ā	âr	är	er	ē	ēr	ī	ō	ŏŏ	ôr	ow	oy	ū	zh	ə
day	air	far	her	bee	tear	light	rope	book	for	cow	boy	tune	vision	item

Day 1

1. ______________________ ☐
2. ______________________ ☐
3. ______________________ ☐
4. ______________________ ☐
5. ______________________ ☐
6. ______________________ ☐
7. ______________________ ☐
8. ______________________ ☐
9. ______________________ ☐
10. ______________________ ☐
11. ______________________ ☐
12. ______________________ ☐
13. ______________________ ☐
14. ______________________ ☐
15. ______________________ ☐
16. ______________________ ☐
17. ______________________ ☐
18. ______________________ ☐
19. ______________________ ☐
20. ______________________ ☐

Day 2

1. ______________________ ☐
2. ______________________ ☐
3. ______________________ ☐
4. ______________________ ☐
5. ______________________ ☐
6. ______________________ ☐
7. ______________________ ☐
8. ______________________ ☐
9. ______________________ ☐
10. ______________________ ☐
11. ______________________ ☐
12. ______________________ ☐
13. ______________________ ☐
14. ______________________ ☐
15. ______________________ ☐
16. ______________________ ☐
17. ______________________ ☐
18. ______________________ ☐
19. ______________________ ☐
20. ______________________ ☐

ā	âr	är	er	ē	ēr	ī	ō	ŏŏ	ôr	ow	oy	ū	zh	ə
day	air	far	her	bee	tear	light	rope	book	for	cow	boy	tune	vision	item

Lesson 5

1.	sak rə men tō	Sacramento	Sac^{3} ra^{2} men^{3} to^{2}	
2.	kal ə fôr nyə	California	Cal^{3} i^{1} for^{3} nia^{3}	
3.	prez ə dent	president	pres^{4} i^{1} dent^{4}	
4.	sen ət	Senate	sen^{3} ate^{3}	
5.	mā yer	mayor	may^{3} or^{2}	Q
6.	sen tins	sentence	sen^{3} tence^{5}	
7.	eks pert	expert	ex^{2} pert^{4}	
8.	eks per tēs	expertise	ex^{2} per^{3} tise^{4}	
9.	mem er ē	memory	mem^{3} or^{2} y^{1}	
10.	kär bən	carbon	car^{3} bon^{3}	
11.	kär bən ā shn	carbonation	car^{3} bon^{3} a^{1} tion^{4}	
12.	prō gram	program	pro^{3} gram^{4}	
13.	pə zi shn	position	po^{2} si^{2} tion^{4}	
14.	fâr well	farewell	fare^{4} well^{4}	
15.	klēnd	cleaned	clean^{5}ed^{2}	J
16.				
17.				
18.				
19.				
20.				

ā	âr	är	er	ē	ēr	ī	ō	ŏŏ	ôr	ow	oy	ū	zh	ə
day	air	far	her	bee	tear	light	rope	book	for	cow	boy	tune	vision	item

Syllable Savvy Spelling Four

Day 3

1. ____________ ☐
2. ____________ ☐
3. ____________ ☐
4. ____________ ☐
5. ____________ ☐
6. ____________ ☐
7. ____________ ☐
8. ____________ ☐
9. ____________ ☐
10. ____________ ☐
11. ____________ ☐
12. ____________ ☐
13. ____________ ☐
14. ____________ ☐
15. ____________ ☐
16. ____________ ☐
17. ____________ ☐
18. ____________ ☐
19. ____________ ☐
20. ____________ ☐

Day 4

1. ____________ ☐
2. ____________ ☐
3. ____________ ☐
4. ____________ ☐
5. ____________ ☐
6. ____________ ☐
7. ____________ ☐
8. ____________ ☐
9. ____________ ☐
10. ____________ ☐
11. ____________ ☐
12. ____________ ☐
13. ____________ ☐
14. ____________ ☐
15. ____________ ☐
16. ____________ ☐
17. ____________ ☐
18. ____________ ☐
19. ____________ ☐
20. ____________ ☐

ā	âr	är	er	ē	ēr	ī	ō	ŏŏ	ôr	ow	oy	ū	zh	ə
day	air	far	her	bee	tear	light	rope	book	for	cow	boy	tune	vision	item

Lesson 5b

1.	sak rə men tō	Sacramento	Sac^{3} ra^{2} men^{3} to^{2}
2.	kal ə fôr nyə	California	Cal^{3} i^{1} for^{3} nia^{3}
3.	prez ə dent	president	pres^{4} i^{1} dent^{4}
4.	sen ət	Senate	sen^{3} ate^{3}
5.	mā yer	mayor	may^{3} or^{2}
6.	sen tins	sentence	sen^{3} tence^{5}
7.	eks pert	expert	ex^{2} pert^{4}
8.	eks per tēs	expertise	ex^{2} per^{3} tise^{4}
9.	mem er ē	memory	mem^{3} or^{2} y^{1}
10.	kär bən	carbon	car^{3} bon^{3}
11.	kär bən ā shn	carbonation	car^{3} bon^{3} a^{1} tion^{4}
12.	prō gram	program	pro^{3} gram^{4}
13.	pə zi shn	position	po^{2} si^{2} tion^{4}
14.	fâr well	farewell	fare^{4} well^{4}
15.	klēnd	cleaned	clean^{5}ed^{2}
16.			
17.			
18.			
19.			
20.			

ā	âr	är	er	ē	ēr	ī	ō	ŏŏ	ôr	ow	oy	ū	zh	ə
day	air	far	her	bee	tear	light	rope	book	for	cow	boy	tune	vision	item

Syllable Savvy Spelling Four

Day 1

1. ____________ ☐
2. ____________ ☐
3. ____________ ☐
4. ____________ ☐
5. ____________ ☐
6. ____________ ☐
7. ____________ ☐
8. ____________ ☐
9. ____________ ☐
10. ____________ ☐
11. ____________ ☐
12. ____________ ☐
13. ____________ ☐
14. ____________ ☐
15. ____________ ☐
16. ____________ ☐
17. ____________ ☐
18. ____________ ☐
19. ____________ ☐
20. ____________ ☐

Day 2

1. ____________ ☐
2. ____________ ☐
3. ____________ ☐
4. ____________ ☐
5. ____________ ☐
6. ____________ ☐
7. ____________ ☐
8. ____________ ☐
9. ____________ ☐
10. ____________ ☐
11. ____________ ☐
12. ____________ ☐
13. ____________ ☐
14. ____________ ☐
15. ____________ ☐
16. ____________ ☐
17. ____________ ☐
18. ____________ ☐
19. ____________ ☐
20. ____________ ☐

ā	âr	är	er	ē	ēr	ī	ō	ŏŏ	ôr	ow	oy	ū	zh	ə
day	air	far	her	bee	tear	light	rope	book	for	cow	boy	tune	vision	item

Lesson 6

1.	den ver	Denver	Den^{3} ver^{3}	
2.	kol ə ra dō	Colorado	Col^{3} o^{1} ra^{2} do^{2}	
3.	tel ə vi zhn	television	tel^{3} e^{1} vi^{2} sion^{4}	
4.	tel ə fōn	telephone	tel^{3} e^{1} phone^{5}	
5.	chärj	charge	charge^{6}	
6.	lo jik	logic	lo^{2} gic^{3}	
7.	lo ji kl	logical	lo^{2} gic^{3} al^{2}	
8.	ster əp	stirrup	stir^{4} rup^{3}	
9.	a sid	acid	a^{1} cid^{3}	
10.	o təm	autumn	au^{2} tumn^{4}	
11.	bē lēf	belief	be^{2} lief^{4}	S
12.	bē lēv	believe	be^{2} lieve^{5}	S
13.	chan nl	channel	chan^{4} nel^{3}	
14.	kən tān	contain	con^{3} tain^{4}	
15.	pen ē les	penniless	pen^{3} ni^{2} less^{4}	C
16.				
17.				
18.				
19.				
20.				

ā	âr	är	er	ē	ēr	ī	ō	ŏŏ	ôr	ow	oy	ū	zh	ə
day	air	far	her	bee	tear	light	rope	book	for	cow	boy	tune	vision	item

Day 3

1. ______________________ ☐
2. ______________________ ☐
3. ______________________ ☐
4. ______________________ ☐
5. ______________________ ☐
6. ______________________ ☐
7. ______________________ ☐
8. ______________________ ☐
9. ______________________ ☐
10. ______________________ ☐
11. ______________________ ☐
12. ______________________ ☐
13. ______________________ ☐
14. ______________________ ☐
15. ______________________ ☐
16. ______________________ ☐
17. ______________________ ☐
18. ______________________ ☐
19. ______________________ ☐
20. ______________________ ☐

Day 4

1. ______________________ ☐
2. ______________________ ☐
3. ______________________ ☐
4. ______________________ ☐
5. ______________________ ☐
6. ______________________ ☐
7. ______________________ ☐
8. ______________________ ☐
9. ______________________ ☐
10. ______________________ ☐
11. ______________________ ☐
12. ______________________ ☐
13. ______________________ ☐
14. ______________________ ☐
15. ______________________ ☐
16. ______________________ ☐
17. ______________________ ☐
18. ______________________ ☐
19. ______________________ ☐
20. ______________________ ☐

ā	âr	är	er	ē	ēr	ī	ō	ŏŏ	ôr	ow	oy	ū	zh	ə
day	air	far	her	bee	tear	light	rope	book	for	cow	boy	tune	vision	item

Lesson 6b

1.	den ver	Denver	Den^3 ver^3
2.	kol ə ra dō	Colorado	Col^3 o^1 ra^2 do^2
3.	tel ə vi zhn	television	tel^3 e^1 vi^2 sion^4
4.	tel ə fōn	telephone	tel^3 e^1 phone^5
5.	chärj	charge	charge^6
6.	lo jik	logic	lo^2 gic^3
7.	lo ji kl	logical	lo^2 gic^3 al^2
8.	ster əp	stirrup	stir^4 rup^3
9.	a sid	acid	a^1 cid^3
10.	o təm	autumn	au^2 tumn^4
11.	bē lēf	belief	be^2 lief^4
12.	bē lēv	believe	be^2 lieve^5
13.	chan nl	channel	chan^4 nel^3
14.	kən tān	contain	con^3 tain^4
15.	pen ē les	penniless	pen^3 ni^2 less^4
16.			
17.			
18.			
19.			
20.			

ā	âr	är	er	ē	ēr	ī	ō	ŏŏ	ôr	ow	oy	ū	zh	ə
day	air	far	her	bee	tear	light	rope	book	for	cow	boy	tune	vision	item

Day 1		Day 2	
1. ______	☐	1. ______	☐
2. ______	☐	2. ______	☐
3. ______	☐	3. ______	☐
4. ______	☐	4. ______	☐
5. ______	☐	5. ______	☐
6. ______	☐	6. ______	☐
7. ______	☐	7. ______	☐
8. ______	☐	8. ______	☐
9. ______	☐	9. ______	☐
10. ______	☐	10. ______	☐
11. ______	☐	11. ______	☐
12. ______	☐	12. ______	☐
13. ______	☐	13. ______	☐
14. ______	☐	14. ______	☐
15. ______	☐	15. ______	☐
16. ______	☐	16. ______	☐
17. ______	☐	17. ______	☐
18. ______	☐	18. ______	☐
19. ______	☐	19. ______	☐
20. ______	☐	20. ______	☐

ā	**âr**	**är**	**er**	**ē**	**ēr**	**ī**	**ō**	**ŏŏ**	**ôr**	**ow**	**oy**	**ū**	**zh**	**ə**
day	air	far	her	bee	tear	light	rope	book	for	cow	boy	tune	vision	item

Lesson 7

1.	**hart ferd**	**Hartford**	**Hart^{4} ford^{4}**	
2.	**ku ne di kət**	**Connecticut**	**Con^{3} nect^{4} i^{1} cut^{3}**	
3.	**kun ekt**	**connect**	**con^{3} nect^{4}**	
4.	**star dəl**	**startle**	**star^{4} tle^{3}**	
5.	**fakt**	**fact**	**fact^{4}**	
6.	**fak ter ē**	**factory**	**fac^{3} tor^{3} y^{1}**	
7.	**plān (flies)**	**plane**	**plane^{5}**	
8.	**plān (simple)**	**plain**	**plain^{5}**	
9.	**eks plān**	**explain**	**ex^{2} plain^{5}**	
10.	**fown dā shn**	**foundation**	**foun^{4} da^{2} tion^{4}**	
11.	**kal i kō**	**calico**	**cal^{3} i^{1} co^{2}**	
12.	**wāt (stop)**	**wait**	**wait^{4}**	
13.	**wāt (heavy)**	**weight**	**weight^{6}**	**S**
14.	**wā**	**weigh**	**weigh^{5}**	**S**
15.	**kul ek tid**	**collected**	**col^{3} lect^{4} ed^{2}**	**J**
16.				
17.				
18.				
19.				
20.				

ā	âr	är	er	ē	ēr	ī	ō	ŏŏ	ôr	ow	oy	ū	zh	ə
day	air	far	her	bee	tear	light	rope	book	for	cow	boy	tune	vision	item

Syllable Savvy Spelling Four

Day 3		Day 4	
1.	☐	1.	☐
2.	☐	2.	☐
3.	☐	3.	☐
4.	☐	4.	☐
5.	☐	5.	☐
6.	☐	6.	☐
7.	☐	7.	☐
8.	☐	8.	☐
9.	☐	9.	☐
10.	☐	10.	☐
11.	☐	11.	☐
12.	☐	12.	☐
13.	☐	13.	☐
14.	☐	14.	☐
15.	☐	15.	☐
16.	☐	16.	☐
17.	☐	17.	☐
18.	☐	18.	☐
19.	☐	19.	☐
20.	☐	20.	☐

ā	**âr**	**är**	**er**	**ē**	**ēr**	**ī**	**ō**	**ŏŏ**	**ôr**	**ow**	**oy**	**ū**	**zh**	**ə**
day	air	far	her	bee	tear	light	rope	book	for	cow	boy	tune	vision	item

Lesson 7b

1.	**hart ferd**	**Hartford**	**Hart^{4} ford^{4}**
2.	**ku ne di kət**	**Connecticut**	**Con^{3} nect^{4} i^{1} cut^{3}**
3.	**kun ekt**	**connect**	**con^{3} nect^{4}**
4.	**star dəl**	**startle**	**star^{4} tle^{3}**
5.	**fakt**	**fact**	**fact^{4}**
6.	**fak ter ē**	**factory**	**fac^{3} tor^{3} y^{1}**
7.	**plān (flies)**	**plane**	**plane^{5}**
8.	**plān (simple)**	**plain**	**plain^{5}**
9.	**eks plān**	**explain**	**ex^{2} plain^{5}**
10.	**fown dā shn**	**foundation**	**foun^{4} da^{2} tion^{4}**
11.	**kal i kō**	**calico**	**cal^{3} i^{1} co^{2}**
12.	**wāt (stop)**	**wait**	**wait^{4}**
13.	**wāt (heavy)**	**weight**	**weight^{6}**
14.	**wā**	**weigh**	**weigh^{5}**
15.	**kul ek tid**	**collected**	**col^{3} lect^{4} ed^{2}**
16.			
17.			
18.			
19.			
20.			

ā	âr	är	er	ē	ēr	ī	ō	ŏŏ	ôr	ow	oy	ū	zh	ə
day	air	far	her	bee	tear	light	rope	book	for	cow	boy	tune	vision	item

Day 1

1. ____________ ☐
2. ____________ ☐
3. ____________ ☐
4. ____________ ☐
5. ____________ ☐
6. ____________ ☐
7. ____________ ☐
8. ____________ ☐
9. ____________ ☐
10. ____________ ☐
11. ____________ ☐
12. ____________ ☐
13. ____________ ☐
14. ____________ ☐
15. ____________ ☐
16. ____________ ☐
17. ____________ ☐
18. ____________ ☐
19. ____________ ☐
20. ____________ ☐

Day 2

1. ____________ ☐
2. ____________ ☐
3. ____________ ☐
4. ____________ ☐
5. ____________ ☐
6. ____________ ☐
7. ____________ ☐
8. ____________ ☐
9. ____________ ☐
10. ____________ ☐
11. ____________ ☐
12. ____________ ☐
13. ____________ ☐
14. ____________ ☐
15. ____________ ☐
16. ____________ ☐
17. ____________ ☐
18. ____________ ☐
19. ____________ ☐
20. ____________ ☐

ā	**âr**	**är**	**er**	**ē**	**ēr**	**ī**	**ō**	**ŏŏ**	**ôr**	**ow**	**oy**	**ū**	**zh**	**ə**
day	air	far	her	bee	tear	light	rope	book	for	cow	boy	tune	vision	item

Lesson 8

1.	dō ver	Dover	Do[2] ver[3]
2.	del ə wâr	Delaware	Del[3] a[1] ware[4]
3.	ə wâr	aware	a[1] ware[4]
4.	per sent	percent	per[3] cent[4]
5.	per sen təj	percentage	per[3] cen[3] tage[4]
6.	av er əj*	average	av[2] er[2] age[3]
7.	in tīr	entire	en[2] tire[4]
8.	sə lekt	select	se[2] lect[4]
9.	sə lek shn	selection	se[2] lec[3] tion[4]
10.	im prūv	improve	im[2] prove[5]
11.	im prūv mint	improvement	im[2] prove[5] ment[4]
12.	thik it	thicket	thick[5] et[2]
13.	wâr (clothes)	wear	wear[4]
14.	wâr (dishes)	ware	ware[4]
15.	whâr (place)	where	where[5]
16.			
17.			
18.			
19.			
20.			

G

ā	âr	är	er	ē	ēr	ī	ō	ŏŏ	ôr	ow	oy	ū	zh	ə
day	air	far	her	bee	tear	light	rope	book	for	cow	boy	tune	vision	item

Syllable Savvy Spelling Four

Day 1		Day 2	
1. ________	☐	1. ________	☐
2. ________	☐	2. ________	☐
3. ________	☐	3. ________	☐
4. ________	☐	4. ________	☐
5. ________	☐	5. ________	☐
6. ________	☐	6. ________	☐
7. ________	☐	7. ________	☐
8. ________	☐	8. ________	☐
9. ________	☐	9. ________	☐
10. ________	☐	10. ________	☐
11. ________	☐	11. ________	☐
12. ________	☐	12. ________	☐
13. ________	☐	13. ________	☐
14. ________	☐	14. ________	☐
15. ________	☐	15. ________	☐
16. ________	☐	16. ________	☐
17. ________	☐	17. ________	☐
18. ________	☐	18. ________	☐
19. ________	☐	19. ________	☐
20. ________	☐	20. ________	☐

ā	**âr**	**är**	**er**	**ē**	**ēr**	**ī**	**ō**	**ŏŏ**	**ôr**	**ow**	**oy**	**ū**	**zh**	**ə**
day	air	far	her	bee	tear	light	rope	book	for	cow	boy	tune	vision	item

Lesson 8b

1.	dō ver	Dover	Do^{2} ver^{3}
2.	del ə wâr	Delaware	Del^{3} a^{1} ware^{4}
3.	ə wâr	aware	a^{1} ware^{4}
4.	per sent	percent	per^{3} cent^{4}
5.	per sen təj	percentage	per^{3} cen^{3} tage^{4}
6.	av er əj*	average	av^{2} er^{2} age^{3}
7.	in tīr	entire	en^{2} tire^{4}
8.	sə lekt	select	se^{2} lect^{4}
9.	sə lek shn	selection	se^{2} lec^{3} tion^{4}
10.	im prūv	improve	im^{2} prove^{5}
11.	im prūv mint	improvement	im^{2} prove^{5} ment^{4}
12.	thik it	thicket	thick^{5} et^{2}
13.	wâr (clothes)	wear	wear^{4}
14.	wâr (dishes)	ware	ware^{4}
15.	whâr (place)	where	where^{5}
16.			
17.			
18.			
19.			
20.			

ā	âr	är	er	ē	ēr	ī	ō	ŏŏ	ôr	ow	oy	ū	zh	ə
day	air	far	her	bee	tear	light	rope	book	for	cow	boy	tune	vision	item

Syllable Savvy Spelling Four

Day 1

1. ____________________ ☐
2. ____________________ ☐
3. ____________________ ☐
4. ____________________ ☐
5. ____________________ ☐
6. ____________________ ☐
7. ____________________ ☐
8. ____________________ ☐
9. ____________________ ☐
10. ____________________ ☐
11. ____________________ ☐
12. ____________________ ☐
13. ____________________ ☐
14. ____________________ ☐
15. ____________________ ☐
16. ____________________ ☐
17. ____________________ ☐
18. ____________________ ☐
19. ____________________ ☐
20. ____________________ ☐

Day 2

1. ____________________ ☐
2. ____________________ ☐
3. ____________________ ☐
4. ____________________ ☐
5. ____________________ ☐
6. ____________________ ☐
7. ____________________ ☐
8. ____________________ ☐
9. ____________________ ☐
10. ____________________ ☐
11. ____________________ ☐
12. ____________________ ☐
13. ____________________ ☐
14. ____________________ ☐
15. ____________________ ☐
16. ____________________ ☐
17. ____________________ ☐
18. ____________________ ☐
19. ____________________ ☐
20. ____________________ ☐

ā	**âr**	**är**	**er**	**ē**	**ēr**	**ī**	**ō**	**ŏŏ**	**ôr**	**ow**	**oy**	**ū**	**zh**	**ə**
day	air	far	her	bee	tear	light	rope	book	for	cow	boy	tune	vision	item

Lesson 9

1.	tal lə ha sē	Tallahassee	Tal^3 la^2 has^3 see^3	
2.	flor i də	Florida	Flor^4 i^1 da^2	
3.	ə rith mə tik	arithmetic	a^1 rith^4 me^2 tic^3	
4.	math ə ma tiks	mathematics	math^4 e^1 ma^2 tics^4	
5.	sē krit	secret	se^2 cret^4	L
6.	giv ən	given	giv^3 en^2	L
7.	sher	sure	sure^4	
8.	sōl (person)	soul	soul^4	
9.	sōl (alone)	sole	sole^4	
10.	ə dop shn	adoption	a^1 dop^3 tion^4	
11.	frē dəm	freedom	free^4 dom^3	
12.	king dəm	kingdom	king^4 dom^3	
13.	də strōy	destroy	de^2 stroy^5	L
14.	də strōyd	destroyed	de^2 stroy^{5}ed^2	J
15.	də struk shn	destruction	de^2 struc^5 tion^4	
16.				
17.				
18.				
19.				
20.				

ā	âr	är	er	ē	ēr	ī	ō	ŏŏ	ôr	ow	oy	ū	zh	ə
day	air	far	her	bee	tear	light	rope	book	for	cow	boy	tune	vision	item

Day 3

1. ______________________ ☐
2. ______________________ ☐
3. ______________________ ☐
4. ______________________ ☐
5. ______________________ ☐
6. ______________________ ☐
7. ______________________ ☐
8. ______________________ ☐
9. ______________________ ☐
10. ______________________ ☐
11. ______________________ ☐
12. ______________________ ☐
13. ______________________ ☐
14. ______________________ ☐
15. ______________________ ☐
16. ______________________ ☐
17. ______________________ ☐
18. ______________________ ☐
19. ______________________ ☐
20. ______________________ ☐

Day 4

1. ______________________ ☐
2. ______________________ ☐
3. ______________________ ☐
4. ______________________ ☐
5. ______________________ ☐
6. ______________________ ☐
7. ______________________ ☐
8. ______________________ ☐
9. ______________________ ☐
10. ______________________ ☐
11. ______________________ ☐
12. ______________________ ☐
13. ______________________ ☐
14. ______________________ ☐
15. ______________________ ☐
16. ______________________ ☐
17. ______________________ ☐
18. ______________________ ☐
19. ______________________ ☐
20. ______________________ ☐

ā	**âr**	**är**	**er**	**ē**	**ēr**	**ī**	**ō**	**ŏŏ**	**ôr**	**ow**	**oy**	**ū**	**zh**	**ə**
day	air	far	her	bee	tear	light	rope	book	for	cow	boy	tune	vision	item

Lesson 9b

1.	tal lə ha sē	Tallahassee	Tal^{3} la^{2} has^{3} see^{3}
2.	flor i də	Florida	Flor^{4} i^{1} da^{2}
3.	ə rith mə tik	arithmetic	a^{1} rith^{4} me^{2} tic^{3}
4.	math ə ma tiks	mathematics	math^{4} e^{1} ma^{2} tics^{4}
5.	sē krit	secret	se^{2} cret^{4}
6.	giv ən	given	giv^{3} en^{2}
7.	sher	sure	sure^{4}
8.	sōl (person)	soul	soul^{4}
9.	sōl (alone)	sole	sole^{4}
10.	ə dop shn	adoption	a^{1} dop^{3} tion^{4}
11.	frē dəm	freedom	free^{4} dom^{3}
12.	king dəm	kingdom	king^{4} dom^{3}
13.	də strōy	destroy	de^{2} stroy^{5}
14.	də strōyd	destroyed	de^{2} stroy^{5}ed^{2}
15.	də struk shn	destruction	de^{2} struc^{5} tion^{4}
16.			
17.			
18.			
19.			
20.			

ā	âr	är	er	ē	ēr	ī	ō	ŏŏ	ôr	ow	oy	ū	zh	ə
day	air	far	her	bee	tear	light	rope	book	for	cow	boy	tune	vision	item

Day 1

1. ______________________ ☐
2. ______________________ ☐
3. ______________________ ☐
4. ______________________ ☐
5. ______________________ ☐
6. ______________________ ☐
7. ______________________ ☐
8. ______________________ ☐
9. ______________________ ☐
10. ______________________ ☐
11. ______________________ ☐
12. ______________________ ☐
13. ______________________ ☐
14. ______________________ ☐
15. ______________________ ☐
16. ______________________ ☐
17. ______________________ ☐
18. ______________________ ☐
19. ______________________ ☐
20. ______________________ ☐

Day 2

1. ______________________ ☐
2. ______________________ ☐
3. ______________________ ☐
4. ______________________ ☐
5. ______________________ ☐
6. ______________________ ☐
7. ______________________ ☐
8. ______________________ ☐
9. ______________________ ☐
10. ______________________ ☐
11. ______________________ ☐
12. ______________________ ☐
13. ______________________ ☐
14. ______________________ ☐
15. ______________________ ☐
16. ______________________ ☐
17. ______________________ ☐
18. ______________________ ☐
19. ______________________ ☐
20. ______________________ ☐

ā	âr	är	er	ē	ēr	ī	ō	ŏŏ	ôr	ow	oy	ū	zh	ə
day	air	far	her	bee	tear	light	rope	book	for	cow	boy	tune	vision	item

Lesson 10

1.	at lan tə	Atlanta	At^2 lan^3 ta^2
2.	jôr jə	Georgia	Geor^4 gia^3
3.	ē gl	eagle	ea^2 gle^3
4.	ə rang ə tang	orangutan	o^1 rang^4 u^1 tan^3
5.	gə ril lə	gorilla	go^2 ril^3 la^2
6.	el ə fənt	elephant	el^2 e^1 phant^5
7.	kang ə rū	kangaroo	kang^4 a^1 roo^3
8.	jer af	giraffe	gir^3 affe^4
9.	flə ming ō	flamingo	fla^3 min^3 go^2
10.	ping win	penguin	pen^3 guin^4
11.	chim pan zē	chimpanzee	chim^4 pan^3 zee^3
12.	lē ō pard*	leopard	leo^3 pard^4
13.	myūl	mule	mule^4
14.	os trij	ostrich	os^2 trich^5
15.	an tə lōp	antelope	an^2 te^2 lope^4
16.			
17.			
18.			
19.			
20.			

G

ā	âr	är	er	ē	ēr	ī	ō	ŏŏ	ôr	ow	oy	ū	zh	ə
day	air	far	her	bee	tear	light	rope	book	for	cow	boy	tune	vision	item

Day 3

1. ______________ ☐
2. ______________ ☐
3. ______________ ☐
4. ______________ ☐
5. ______________ ☐
6. ______________ ☐
7. ______________ ☐
8. ______________ ☐
9. ______________ ☐
10. ______________ ☐
11. ______________ ☐
12. ______________ ☐
13. ______________ ☐
14. ______________ ☐
15. ______________ ☐
16. ______________ ☐
17. ______________ ☐
18. ______________ ☐
19. ______________ ☐
20. ______________ ☐

Day 4

1. ______________ ☐
2. ______________ ☐
3. ______________ ☐
4. ______________ ☐
5. ______________ ☐
6. ______________ ☐
7. ______________ ☐
8. ______________ ☐
9. ______________ ☐
10. ______________ ☐
11. ______________ ☐
12. ______________ ☐
13. ______________ ☐
14. ______________ ☐
15. ______________ ☐
16. ______________ ☐
17. ______________ ☐
18. ______________ ☐
19. ______________ ☐
20. ______________ ☐

ā	âr	är	er	ē	ēr	ī	ō	ŏŏ	ôr	ow	oy	ū	zh	ə
day	air	far	her	bee	tear	light	rope	book	for	cow	boy	tune	vision	item

Lesson 10b

1.	at lan tə	Atlanta	At^{2} lan^{3} ta^{2}
2.	jôr jə	Georgia	Geor^{4} gia^{3}
3.	ē gl	eagle	ea^{2} gle^{3}
4.	ə rang ə tang	orangutan	o^{1} rang^{4} u^{1} tan^{3}
5.	gə ril lə	gorilla	go^{2} ril^{3} la^{2}
6.	el ə fənt	elephant	el^{2} e^{1} phant^{5}
7.	kang ə rū	kangaroo	kang^{4} a^{1} roo^{3}
8.	jer af	giraffe	gir^{3} affe^{4}
9.	flə ming ō	flamingo	fla^{3} min^{3} go^{2}
10.	ping win	penguin	pen^{3} guin^{4}
11.	chim pan zē	chimpanzee	chim^{4} pan^{3} zee^{3}
12.	le perd	leopard	leo^{3} pard^{4}
13.	myūl	mule	mule^{4}
14.	os trij	ostrich	os^{2} trich^{5}
15.	an tə lōp	antelope	an^{2} te^{2} lope^{4}
16.			
17.			
18.			
19.			
20.			

ā	âr	är	er	ē	ēr	ī	ō	ŏŏ	ôr	ow	oy	ū	zh	ə
day	air	far	her	bee	tear	light	rope	book	for	cow	boy	tune	vision	item

Day 1

1. ____________________ ☐
2. ____________________ ☐
3. ____________________ ☐
4. ____________________ ☐
5. ____________________ ☐
6. ____________________ ☐
7. ____________________ ☐
8. ____________________ ☐
9. ____________________ ☐
10. ____________________ ☐
11. ____________________ ☐
12. ____________________ ☐
13. ____________________ ☐
14. ____________________ ☐
15. ____________________ ☐
16. ____________________ ☐
17. ____________________ ☐
18. ____________________ ☐
19. ____________________ ☐
20. ____________________ ☐

Day 2

1. ____________________ ☐
2. ____________________ ☐
3. ____________________ ☐
4. ____________________ ☐
5. ____________________ ☐
6. ____________________ ☐
7. ____________________ ☐
8. ____________________ ☐
9. ____________________ ☐
10. ____________________ ☐
11. ____________________ ☐
12. ____________________ ☐
13. ____________________ ☐
14. ____________________ ☐
15. ____________________ ☐
16. ____________________ ☐
17. ____________________ ☐
18. ____________________ ☐
19. ____________________ ☐
20. ____________________ ☐

ā	**âr**	**är**	**er**	**ē**	**ēr**	**ī**	**ō**	**ŏŏ**	**ôr**	**ow**	**oy**	**ū**	**zh**	**ə**
day	air	far	her	bee	tear	light	rope	book	for	cow	boy	tune	vision	item

Lesson 11

1.	hon ə lū lū	Honolulu	Hon^{3} o^{1} lu^{2} lu^{2}	
2.	hə wī ē	Hawaii	Ha^{2} wa^{2} ii^{2}	
3.	boy zē	Boise	Boi^{3} se^{2}	
4.	ī də hō	Idaho	I^{1} da^{2} ho^{2}	
5.	thâr (place)	there	there^{5}	
6.	thâr (belongs to them)	their	their^{5}	
7.	thâr (they are)	they're	they^{4} 're^{3}	U
8.	sē zəns	seasons	sea^{3} sons^{4}	
9.	hol i dā	holiday	hol^{3} i^{1} day^{3}	
10.	smūth	smooth	smooth^{6}	
11.	bâr ē	bury	bur^{3} y^{1}	
12.	bâr ē əl	burial	bur^{3} i^{1} al^{2}	C
13.	stāk (meat)	steak	steak^{5}	
14.	stāk (spike in the ground)	stake	stake^{5}	
15.	strēk	streak	streak^{6}	
16.				
17.				
18.				
19.				
20.				

ā	âr	är	er	ē	ēr	ī	ō	ŏŏ	ôr	ow	oy	ū	zh	ə
day	air	far	her	bee	tear	light	rope	book	for	cow	boy	tune	vision	item

Day 3

1. ____________________ ☐
2. ____________________ ☐
3. ____________________ ☐
4. ____________________ ☐
5. ____________________ ☐
6. ____________________ ☐
7. ____________________ ☐
8. ____________________ ☐
9. ____________________ ☐
10. ____________________ ☐
11. ____________________ ☐
12. ____________________ ☐
13. ____________________ ☐
14. ____________________ ☐
15. ____________________ ☐
16. ____________________ ☐
17. ____________________ ☐
18. ____________________ ☐
19. ____________________ ☐
20. ____________________ ☐

Day 4

1. ____________________ ☐
2. ____________________ ☐
3. ____________________ ☐
4. ____________________ ☐
5. ____________________ ☐
6. ____________________ ☐
7. ____________________ ☐
8. ____________________ ☐
9. ____________________ ☐
10. ____________________ ☐
11. ____________________ ☐
12. ____________________ ☐
13. ____________________ ☐
14. ____________________ ☐
15. ____________________ ☐
16. ____________________ ☐
17. ____________________ ☐
18. ____________________ ☐
19. ____________________ ☐
20. ____________________ ☐

ā	âr	är	er	ē	ēr	ī	ō	ŏŏ	ôr	ow	oy	ū	zh	ə
day	air	far	her	bee	tear	light	rope	book	for	cow	boy	tune	vision	item

Lesson 11b

1.	hon ə lū lū	Honolulu	Hon^{3} o^{1} lu^{2} lu^{2}
2.	hə wī ē	Hawaii	Ha^{2} wa^{2} ii^{2}
3.	boy zē	Boise	Boi^{3} se^{2}
4.	ī də hō	Idaho	I^{1} da^{2} ho^{2}
5.	thâr (place)	there	there^{5}
6.	thâr (belongs to them)	their	their^{5}
7.	thâr (they are)	they're	they^{4} ‘re^{3}
8.	sē zəns	seasons	sea^{3} sons^{4}
9.	hol i dā	holiday	hol^{3} i^{1} day^{3}
10.	smūth	smooth	smooth^{6}
11.	bâr ē	bury	bur^{3} y^{1}
12.	bâr ē əl	burial	bur^{3} i^{1} al^{2}
13.	stāk (meat)	steak	steak^{5}
14.	stāk (spike in the ground)	stake	stake^{5}
15.	strēk	streak	streak^{6}
16.			
17.			
18.			
19.			
20.			

ā	âr	är	er	ē	ēr	ī	ō	ŏŏ	ôr	ow	oy	ū	zh	ə
day	air	far	her	bee	tear	light	rope	book	for	cow	boy	tune	vision	item

Day 1

1. ______________________ ☐
2. ______________________ ☐
3. ______________________ ☐
4. ______________________ ☐
5. ______________________ ☐
6. ______________________ ☐
7. ______________________ ☐
8. ______________________ ☐
9. ______________________ ☐
10. ______________________ ☐
11. ______________________ ☐
12. ______________________ ☐
13. ______________________ ☐
14. ______________________ ☐
15. ______________________ ☐
16. ______________________ ☐
17. ______________________ ☐
18. ______________________ ☐
19. ______________________ ☐
20. ______________________ ☐

Day 2

1. ______________________ ☐
2. ______________________ ☐
3. ______________________ ☐
4. ______________________ ☐
5. ______________________ ☐
6. ______________________ ☐
7. ______________________ ☐
8. ______________________ ☐
9. ______________________ ☐
10. ______________________ ☐
11. ______________________ ☐
12. ______________________ ☐
13. ______________________ ☐
14. ______________________ ☐
15. ______________________ ☐
16. ______________________ ☐
17. ______________________ ☐
18. ______________________ ☐
19. ______________________ ☐
20. ______________________ ☐

ā	**âr**	**är**	**er**	**ē**	**ēr**	**ī**	**ō**	**o͝o**	**ôr**	**ow**	**oy**	**ū**	**zh**	**ə**
day	air	far	her	bee	tear	light	rope	book	for	cow	boy	tune	vision	item

Lesson 12

1.	sprēng fēld	Springfield	Spring[6] field[5]
2.	il ə noy	Illinois	Il[2] li[2] nois[4]
3.	in dē ən ap ə lis	Indianapolis	In[2] di[2] an[2] ap[2] o[1] lis[3] **M**
4.	in dē an ə	Indiana	In[2] di[2] an[2] a[1]
5.	ēz	ease	ease[4]
6.	ēz ē	easy	ea[2] sy[2]
7.	ak shū əl	actual	ac[2] tu[2] al[2]
8.	emp tē	empty	emp[3] ty[2]
9.	kum fert	comfort	com[3] fort[4]
10.	kum fer tə bl	comfortable	com[3] fort[4] a[1] ble[3]
11.	pān (ouch)	pain	pain[4]
12.	pān (window glass)	pane	pane[4]
13.	duv	dove	dove[4]
14.	fol in	fallen	fal[3] len[3]
15.	hap ind	happened	hap[3] pen[3]ed[2] **J**
16.			
17.			
18.			
19.			
20.			

ā	âr	är	er	ē	ēr	ī	ō	ŏŏ	ôr	ow	oy	ū	zh	ə
day	air	far	her	bee	tear	light	rope	book	for	cow	boy	tune	vision	item

Syllable Savvy Spelling Four

Day 3

1. ______________________ ☐
2. ______________________ ☐
3. ______________________ ☐
4. ______________________ ☐
5. ______________________ ☐
6. ______________________ ☐
7. ______________________ ☐
8. ______________________ ☐
9. ______________________ ☐
10. ______________________ ☐
11. ______________________ ☐
12. ______________________ ☐
13. ______________________ ☐
14. ______________________ ☐
15. ______________________ ☐
16. ______________________ ☐
17. ______________________ ☐
18. ______________________ ☐
19. ______________________ ☐
20. ______________________ ☐

Day 4

1. ______________________ ☐
2. ______________________ ☐
3. ______________________ ☐
4. ______________________ ☐
5. ______________________ ☐
6. ______________________ ☐
7. ______________________ ☐
8. ______________________ ☐
9. ______________________ ☐
10. ______________________ ☐
11. ______________________ ☐
12. ______________________ ☐
13. ______________________ ☐
14. ______________________ ☐
15. ______________________ ☐
16. ______________________ ☐
17. ______________________ ☐
18. ______________________ ☐
19. ______________________ ☐
20. ______________________ ☐

ā	**âr**	**är**	**er**	**ē**	**ēr**	**ī**	**ō**	**ŏŏ**	**ôr**	**ow**	**oy**	**ū**	**zh**	**ə**
day	air	far	her	bee	tear	light	rope	book	for	cow	boy	tune	vision	item

Lesson 12b

1.	sprēng fēld	Springfield	Spring^{6} field^{5}
2.	il ə noy	Illinois	Il^{2} li^{2} nois^{4}
3.	in dē ən ap ə lis	Indianapolis	In^{2} di^{2} an^{2} ap^{2} o^{1} lis^{3}
4.	in dē an ə	Indiana	In^{2} di^{2} an^{2} a^{1}
5.	ēz	ease	ease^{4}
6.	ēz ē	easy	ea^{2} sy^{2}
7.	ak shū əl	actual	ac^{2} tu^{2} al^{2}
8.	emp tē	empty	emp^{3} ty^{2}
9.	kum fert	comfort	com^{3} fort^{4}
10.	kum fer tə bl	comfortable	com^{3} fort^{4} a^{1} ble^{3}
11.	pān (ouch)	pain	pain^{4}
12.	pān (window glass)	pane	pane^{4}
13.	duv	dove	dove^{4}
14.	fol in	fallen	fal^{3} len^{3}
15.	hap ind	happened	hap^{3} pen^{3}ed^{2}
16.			
17.			
18.			
19.			
20.			

ā	âr	är	er	ē	ēr	ī	ō	ŏŏ	ôr	ow	oy	ū	zh	ə
day	air	far	her	bee	tear	light	rope	book	for	cow	boy	tune	vision	item

Syllable Savvy Spelling Four

Day 1

1. ______________ ☐
2. ______________ ☐
3. ______________ ☐
4. ______________ ☐
5. ______________ ☐
6. ______________ ☐
7. ______________ ☐
8. ______________ ☐
9. ______________ ☐
10. ______________ ☐
11. ______________ ☐
12. ______________ ☐
13. ______________ ☐
14. ______________ ☐
15. ______________ ☐
16. ______________ ☐
17. ______________ ☐
18. ______________ ☐
19. ______________ ☐
20. ______________ ☐

Day 2

1. ______________ ☐
2. ______________ ☐
3. ______________ ☐
4. ______________ ☐
5. ______________ ☐
6. ______________ ☐
7. ______________ ☐
8. ______________ ☐
9. ______________ ☐
10. ______________ ☐
11. ______________ ☐
12. ______________ ☐
13. ______________ ☐
14. ______________ ☐
15. ______________ ☐
16. ______________ ☐
17. ______________ ☐
18. ______________ ☐
19. ______________ ☐
20. ______________ ☐

ā	**âr**	**är**	**er**	**ē**	**ēr**	**ī**	**ō**	**ŏŏ**	**ôr**	**ow**	**oy**	**ū**	**zh**	**ə**
day	air	far	her	bee	tear	light	rope	book	for	cow	boy	tune	vision	item

Lesson 13

1.	də moyn	Des Moines	Des^{3} Moines^{6}
2	ī ə wə	Iowa	I^{1} o^{1} wa^{2}
3.	tə pē kə	Topeka	To^{2} pe^{2} ka^{2}
4.	kan zəs	Kansas	Kan^{3} sas^{3}
5.	val en tīn	valentine	val^{3} en^{2} tine^{4}
6.	nūz pā per	newspaper	news^{4} pa^{2} per^{3}
7.	ef ert	effort	ef^{2} fort^{4}
8.	myū zik	music	mu^{2} sic^{3}
9.	myū zik əl	musical	mu^{2} sic^{3} al^{2}
10.	kâr ēn	caring	car^{3} ing^{3}
11.	wol it	wallet	wal^{3} let^{3}
12.	wiz dəm	wisdom	wis^{3} dom^{3}
13.	tu nl	tunnel	tun^{3} nel^{3}
14.	jen er ā shn	generation	gen^{3} er^{2} a^{1} tion^{4}
15.	ī den ti fī	identify	i^{1} den^{3} ti^{2} fy^{2}
16.			
17.			
18.			
19.			
20.			

H

ā	âr	är	er	ē	ēr	ī	ō	ŏŏ	ôr	ow	oy	ū	zh	ə
day	air	far	her	bee	tear	light	rope	book	for	cow	boy	tune	vision	item

Day 3

1. ______________________ ☐
2. ______________________ ☐
3. ______________________ ☐
4. ______________________ ☐
5. ______________________ ☐
6. ______________________ ☐
7. ______________________ ☐
8. ______________________ ☐
9. ______________________ ☐
10. ______________________ ☐
11. ______________________ ☐
12. ______________________ ☐
13. ______________________ ☐
14. ______________________ ☐
15. ______________________ ☐
16. ______________________ ☐
17. ______________________ ☐
18. ______________________ ☐
19. ______________________ ☐
20. ______________________ ☐

Day 4

1. ______________________ ☐
2. ______________________ ☐
3. ______________________ ☐
4. ______________________ ☐
5. ______________________ ☐
6. ______________________ ☐
7. ______________________ ☐
8. ______________________ ☐
9. ______________________ ☐
10. ______________________ ☐
11. ______________________ ☐
12. ______________________ ☐
13. ______________________ ☐
14. ______________________ ☐
15. ______________________ ☐
16. ______________________ ☐
17. ______________________ ☐
18. ______________________ ☐
19. ______________________ ☐
20. ______________________ ☐

ā	**âr**	**är**	**er**	**ē**	**ēr**	**ī**	**ō**	**ŏŏ**	**ôr**	**ow**	**oy**	**ū**	**zh**	**ə**
day	air	far	her	bee	tear	light	rope	book	for	cow	boy	tune	vision	item

Lesson 13b

1.	**də moyn**	**Des Moines**	**Des^{3} Moines^{6}**
2	**ī ə wə**	**Iowa**	**I^{1} o^{1} wa^{2}**
3.	**tə pē kə**	**Topeka**	**To^{2} pe^{2} ka^{2}**
4.	**kan zəs**	**Kansas**	**Kan^{3} sas^{3}**
5.	**val en tīn**	**valentine**	**val^{3} en^{2} tine^{4}**
6.	**nūz pā per**	**newspaper**	**news^{4} pa^{2} per^{3}**
7.	**ef ert**	**effort**	**ef^{2} fort^{4}**
8.	**myū zik**	**music**	**mu^{2} sic^{3}**
9.	**myū zik əl**	**musical**	**mu^{2} sic^{3} al^{2}**
10.	**kâr ēn**	**caring**	**car^{3} ing^{3}**
11.	**wol it**	**wallet**	**wal^{3} let^{3}**
12.	**wiz dəm**	**wisdom**	**wis^{3} dom^{3}**
13.	**tu nl**	**tunnel**	**tun^{3} nel^{3}**
14.	**jen er ā shn**	**generation**	**gen^{3} er^{2} a^{1} tion^{4}**
15.	**ī den ti fī**	**identify**	**i^{1} den^{3} ti^{2} fy^{2}**
16.			
17.			
18.			
19.			
20.			

ā	âr	är	er	ē	ēr	ī	ō	ŏŏ	ôr	ow	oy	ū	zh	ə
day	air	far	her	bee	tear	light	rope	book	for	cow	boy	tune	vision	item

Day 1

1. ______________________ ☐
2. ______________________ ☐
3. ______________________ ☐
4. ______________________ ☐
5. ______________________ ☐
6. ______________________ ☐
7. ______________________ ☐
8. ______________________ ☐
9. ______________________ ☐
10. ______________________ ☐
11. ______________________ ☐
12. ______________________ ☐
13. ______________________ ☐
14. ______________________ ☐
15. ______________________ ☐
16. ______________________ ☐
17. ______________________ ☐
18. ______________________ ☐
19. ______________________ ☐
20. ______________________ ☐

Day 2

1. ______________________ ☐
2. ______________________ ☐
3. ______________________ ☐
4. ______________________ ☐
5. ______________________ ☐
6. ______________________ ☐
7. ______________________ ☐
8. ______________________ ☐
9. ______________________ ☐
10. ______________________ ☐
11. ______________________ ☐
12. ______________________ ☐
13. ______________________ ☐
14. ______________________ ☐
15. ______________________ ☐
16. ______________________ ☐
17. ______________________ ☐
18. ______________________ ☐
19. ______________________ ☐
20. ______________________ ☐

ā	**âr**	**är**	**er**	**ē**	**ēr**	**ī**	**ō**	**ŏŏ**	**ôr**	**ow**	**oy**	**ū**	**zh**	**ə**
day	air	far	her	bee	tear	light	rope	book	for	cow	boy	tune	vision	item

Lesson 14

1.	frank fert	Frankfort	Frank^{5} fort^{4}	
2.	ken tuk ē	Kentucky	Ken^{3} tuck^{4} y^{1}	
3.	bat in rūj	Baton Rouge	Bat^{3} on^{2} Rouge^{5}	
4	lū wē zē an ə	Louisiana	Lou^{3} i^{1} si^{2} an^{2} a^{1}	M
5.	ē fek tiv	effective	ef^{2} fec^{3} tive^{4}	
6.	plush	plush	plush^{5}	
7.	skwēz	squeeze	squeeze^{7}	
8.	skāt	skate	skate^{5}	
9.	zōn	zone	zone^{4}	
10.	prīd	pride	pride^{5}	
11.	prowd	proud	proud^{5}	
12.	kôr	core	core^{4}	
13.	bī	buy	buy^{3}	
14.	bot	bought	bought^{6}	O
15.	här vist	harvest	har^{3} vest^{4}	
16.				
17.				
18.				
19.				
20.				

ā	âr	är	er	ē	ēr	ī	ō	ŏŏ	ôr	ow	oy	ū	zh	ə
day	air	far	her	bee	tear	light	rope	book	for	cow	boy	tune	vision	item

Day 3

1. ______________ ☐
2. ______________ ☐
3. ______________ ☐
4. ______________ ☐
5. ______________ ☐
6. ______________ ☐
7. ______________ ☐
8. ______________ ☐
9. ______________ ☐
10. ______________ ☐
11. ______________ ☐
12. ______________ ☐
13. ______________ ☐
14. ______________ ☐
15. ______________ ☐
16. ______________ ☐
17. ______________ ☐
18. ______________ ☐
19. ______________ ☐
20. ______________ ☐

Day 4

1. ______________ ☐
2. ______________ ☐
3. ______________ ☐
4. ______________ ☐
5. ______________ ☐
6. ______________ ☐
7. ______________ ☐
8. ______________ ☐
9. ______________ ☐
10. ______________ ☐
11. ______________ ☐
12. ______________ ☐
13. ______________ ☐
14. ______________ ☐
15. ______________ ☐
16. ______________ ☐
17. ______________ ☐
18. ______________ ☐
19. ______________ ☐
20. ______________ ☐

ā	âr	är	er	ē	ēr	ī	ō	ŏŏ	ôr	ow	oy	ū	zh	ə
day	air	far	her	bee	tear	light	rope	book	for	cow	boy	tune	vision	item

Lesson 14b

1.	frank fert	Frankfort	Frank^{5} fort^{4}
2.	ken tuk ē	Kentucky	Ken^{3} tuck^{4} y^{1}
3.	bat in rūj	Baton Rouge	Bat^{3} on^{2} Rouge^{5}
4	lū wē zē an ə	Louisiana	Lou^{3} i^{1} si^{2} an^{2} a^{1}
5.	ē fek tiv	effective	ef^{2} fec^{3} tive^{4}
6.	plush	plush	plush^{5}
7.	skwēz	squeeze	squeeze^{7}
8.	skāt	skate	skate^{5}
9.	zōn	zone	zone^{4}
10.	prīd	pride	pride^{5}
11.	prowd	proud	proud^{5}
12.	kôr	core	core^{4}
13.	bī	buy	buy^{3}
14.	bot	bought	bought^{6}
15.	här vist	harvest	har^{3} vest^{4}
16.			
17.			
18.			
19.			
20.			

ā	âr	är	er	ē	ēr	ī	ō	ŏŏ	ôr	ow	oy	ū	zh	ə
day	air	far	her	bee	tear	light	rope	book	for	cow	boy	tune	vision	item

Syllable Savvy Spelling Four

Day 1

1. ____________ ☐
2. ____________ ☐
3. ____________ ☐
4. ____________ ☐
5. ____________ ☐
6. ____________ ☐
7. ____________ ☐
8. ____________ ☐
9. ____________ ☐
10. ____________ ☐
11. ____________ ☐
12. ____________ ☐
13. ____________ ☐
14. ____________ ☐
15. ____________ ☐
16. ____________ ☐
17. ____________ ☐
18. ____________ ☐
19. ____________ ☐
20. ____________ ☐

Day 2

1. ____________ ☐
2. ____________ ☐
3. ____________ ☐
4. ____________ ☐
5. ____________ ☐
6. ____________ ☐
7. ____________ ☐
8. ____________ ☐
9. ____________ ☐
10. ____________ ☐
11. ____________ ☐
12. ____________ ☐
13. ____________ ☐
14. ____________ ☐
15. ____________ ☐
16. ____________ ☐
17. ____________ ☐
18. ____________ ☐
19. ____________ ☐
20. ____________ ☐

ā	**âr**	**är**	**er**	**ē**	**ēr**	**ī**	**ō**	**ŏŏ**	**ôr**	**ow**	**oy**	**ū**	**zh**	**ə**
day	air	far	her	bee	tear	light	rope	book	for	cow	boy	tune	vision	item

Lesson 15

1.	u gus tə	Augusta	Au^2 gus^3 ta^2	
2	mān	Maine	Maine^5	
3.	an nap ə lis	Annapolis	An^2 nap^3 o^1 lis^3	
4.	mâr i lind	Maryland	Mar^3 y^1 land^4	
5.	chīld hŏŏd	childhood	child^5 hood^4	
6.	in fôrmd	informed	in^2 form^{4}ed^2	J
7.	flā verd	flavored	fla^3 vor^{3}ed^2	J
8.	rē kwest	request	re^2 quest^5	
9.	drī yer (machine)	dryer	dry^3 er^2	
10.	drī yer (less wet)	drier	dri^3 er^2	C
11.	frī tind	frightened	fright^6 en^{2}ed^2	N
12.	thow zind	thousand	thou^4 sand^4	
13.	hun drid	hundred	hun^3 dred^4	
14.	mil yin	million	mil^3 lion^4	
15.	bil yin	billion	bil^3 lion^4	
16.				
17.				
18.				
19.				
20.				

ā	âr	är	er	ē	ēr	ī	ō	ŏŏ	ôr	ow	oy	ū	zh	ə
day	air	far	her	bee	tear	light	rope	book	for	cow	boy	tune	vision	item

Day 3		Day 4	
1.	☐	1.	☐
2.	☐	2.	☐
3.	☐	3.	☐
4.	☐	4.	☐
5.	☐	5.	☐
6.	☐	6.	☐
7.	☐	7.	☐
8.	☐	8.	☐
9.	☐	9.	☐
10.	☐	10.	☐
11.	☐	11.	☐
12.	☐	12.	☐
13.	☐	13.	☐
14.	☐	14.	☐
15.	☐	15.	☐
16.	☐	16.	☐
17.	☐	17.	☐
18.	☐	18.	☐
19.	☐	19.	☐
20.	☐	20.	☐

ā	**âr**	**är**	**er**	**ē**	**ēr**	**ī**	**ō**	**ŏŏ**	**ôr**	**ow**	**oy**	**ū**	**zh**	**ə**
day	air	far	her	bee	tear	light	rope	book	for	cow	boy	tune	vision	item

Lesson 15b

1.	**u gus tə**	**Augusta**	**Au^{2} gus^{3} ta^{2}**
2	**mān**	**Maine**	**Maine^{5}**
3.	**an nap ə lis**	**Annapolis**	**An^{2} nap^{3} o^{1} lis^{3}**
4.	**mâr i lind**	**Maryland**	**Mar^{3} y^{1} land^{4}**
5.	**chīld hŏŏd**	**childhood**	**child^{5} hood^{4}**
6.	**in fôrmd**	**informed**	**in^{2} form^{4}ed^{2}**
7.	**flā verd**	**flavored**	**fla^{3} vor^{3}ed^{2}**
8.	**rē kwest**	**request**	**re^{2} quest^{5}**
9.	**drī yer (machine)**	**dryer**	**dry^{3} er^{2}**
10.	**drī yer (less wet)**	**drier**	**dri^{3} er^{2}**
11.	**frī tind**	**frightened**	**fright^{6} en^{2}ed^{2}**
12.	**thow zind**	**thousand**	**thou^{4} sand^{4}**
13.	**hun drid**	**hundred**	**hun^{3} dred^{4}**
14.	**mil yin**	**million**	**mil^{3} lion^{4}**
15.	**bil yin**	**billion**	**bil^{3} lion^{4}**
16.			
17.			
18.			
19.			
20.			

ā	**âr**	**är**	**er**	**ē**	**ēr**	**ī**	**ō**	**ŏŏ**	**ôr**	**ow**	**oy**	**ū**	**zh**	**ə**
day	air	far	her	bee	tear	light	rope	book	for	cow	boy	tune	vision	item

Syllable Savvy Spelling Four

Day 1		Day 2	
1.	☐	1.	☐
2.	☐	2.	☐
3.	☐	3.	☐
4.	☐	4.	☐
5.	☐	5.	☐
6.	☐	6.	☐
7.	☐	7.	☐
8.	☐	8.	☐
9.	☐	9.	☐
10.	☐	10.	☐
11.	☐	11.	☐
12.	☐	12.	☐
13.	☐	13.	☐
14.	☐	14.	☐
15.	☐	15.	☐
16.	☐	16.	☐
17.	☐	17.	☐
18.	☐	18.	☐
19.	☐	19.	☐
20.	☐	20.	☐

ā	âr	är	er	ē	ēr	ī	ō	ŏŏ	ôr	ow	oy	ū	zh	ə
day	air	far	her	bee	tear	light	rope	book	for	cow	boy	tune	vision	item

Lesson 16

1.	bos tən	Boston	Bos^{3} ton^{3}	
2.	mas sə chū sits	Massachusetts	Mas^{3} sa^{2} chu^{3} setts^{5}	
3.	lan sēn	Lansing	Lan^{3} sing^{4}	
4.	mi shi gən	Michigan	Mi^{2} chi^{3} gan^{3}	
5.	fôr werd	forward	for^{3} ward^{4}	R
6.	per ād	parade	par^{3} ade^{3}	
7.	ser prīz	surprise	sur^{3} prise^{5}	
8.	eks plōr erz	explorers	ex^{2} plor^{4} ers^{3}	I
9.	âr ō	arrow	ar^{2} row^{3}	
10.	dis kuv er	discover	dis^{3} cov^{3} er^{2}	
11.	trans fer	transfer	trans^{5} fer^{3}	
12.	owt lŏŏk	outlook	out^{3} look^{4}	
13.	a di tūd	attitude	at^{2} ti^{2} tude^{4}	
14.	tə wôrdz	towards	to^{2} wards^{5}	
15.	in fənt	infant	in^{2} fant^{4}	
16.				
17.				
18.				
19.				
20.				

ā	âr	är	er	ē	ēr	ī	ō	ŏŏ	ôr	ow	oy	ū	zh	ə
day	air	far	her	bee	tear	light	rope	book	for	cow	boy	tune	vision	item

Syllable Savvy Spelling Four

Day 3

1. ____________ ☐
2. ____________ ☐
3. ____________ ☐
4. ____________ ☐
5. ____________ ☐
6. ____________ ☐
7. ____________ ☐
8. ____________ ☐
9. ____________ ☐
10. ____________ ☐
11. ____________ ☐
12. ____________ ☐
13. ____________ ☐
14. ____________ ☐
15. ____________ ☐
16. ____________ ☐
17. ____________ ☐
18. ____________ ☐
19. ____________ ☐
20. ____________ ☐

Day 4

1. ____________ ☐
2. ____________ ☐
3. ____________ ☐
4. ____________ ☐
5. ____________ ☐
6. ____________ ☐
7. ____________ ☐
8. ____________ ☐
9. ____________ ☐
10. ____________ ☐
11. ____________ ☐
12. ____________ ☐
13. ____________ ☐
14. ____________ ☐
15. ____________ ☐
16. ____________ ☐
17. ____________ ☐
18. ____________ ☐
19. ____________ ☐
20. ____________ ☐

ā	**âr**	**är**	**er**	**ē**	**ēr**	**ī**	**ō**	**ŏŏ**	**ôr**	**ow**	**oy**	**ū**	**zh**	**ə**
day	air	far	her	bee	tear	light	rope	book	for	cow	boy	tune	vision	item

Lesson 16b

1.	bos tən	Boston	Bos^3 ton^3
2.	mas sə chū sits	Massachusetts	Mas^3 sa^2 chu^3 setts^5
3.	lan sēn	Lansing	Lan^3 sing^4
4.	mi shi gən	Michigan	Mi^2 chi^3 gan^3
5.	fôr werd	forward	for^3 ward^4
6.	per ād	parade	par^3 ade^3
7.	ser prīz	surprise	sur^3 prise^5
8.	eks plōr erz	explorers	ex^2 plor^4 ers^3
9.	âr ō	arrow	ar^2 row^3
10.	dis kuv er	discover	dis^3 cov^3 er^2
11.	trans fer	transfer	trans^5 fer^3
12.	owt lŏŏk	outlook	out^3 look^4
13.	a di tūd	attitude	at^2 ti^2 tude^4
14.	tə wôrdz	towards	to^2 wards^5
15.	in fənt	infant	in^2 fant^4
16.			
17.			
18.			
19.			
20.			

ā	âr	är	er	ē	ēr	ī	ō	ŏŏ	ôr	ow	oy	ū	zh	ə
day	air	far	her	bee	tear	light	rope	book	for	cow	boy	tune	vision	item

Day 1

1. ____________________ ☐
2. ____________________ ☐
3. ____________________ ☐
4. ____________________ ☐
5. ____________________ ☐
6. ____________________ ☐
7. ____________________ ☐
8. ____________________ ☐
9. ____________________ ☐
10. ____________________ ☐
11. ____________________ ☐
12. ____________________ ☐
13. ____________________ ☐
14. ____________________ ☐
15. ____________________ ☐
16. ____________________ ☐
17. ____________________ ☐
18. ____________________ ☐
19. ____________________ ☐
20. ____________________ ☐

Day 2

1. ____________________ ☐
2. ____________________ ☐
3. ____________________ ☐
4. ____________________ ☐
5. ____________________ ☐
6. ____________________ ☐
7. ____________________ ☐
8. ____________________ ☐
9. ____________________ ☐
10. ____________________ ☐
11. ____________________ ☐
12. ____________________ ☐
13. ____________________ ☐
14. ____________________ ☐
15. ____________________ ☐
16. ____________________ ☐
17. ____________________ ☐
18. ____________________ ☐
19. ____________________ ☐
20. ____________________ ☐

ā	**âr**	**är**	**er**	**ē**	**ēr**	**ī**	**ō**	**ŏŏ**	**ôr**	**ow**	**oy**	**ū**	**zh**	**ə**
day	air	far	her	bee	tear	light	rope	book	for	cow	boy	tune	vision	item

Lesson 17

1.	sānt pol	Saint Paul	Saint^{5} Paul^{4}	
2	Min nə sō də	Minnesota	Min^{3} ne^{2} so^{2} ta^{2}	
3.	jak sən	Jackson	Jack^{4} son^{3}	
4.	mis sə sip pē	Mississippi	Mis^{3} sis^{3} sip^{3} pi^{2}	
5.	är tis tik	artistic	ar^{2} tis^{3} tic^{3}	
6.	thank ful	thankful	thank^{5} ful^{3}	
7.	gra di tūd	gratitude	grat^{4} i^{1} tude^{4}	
8.	klow did	clouded	clou^{4} ded^{3}	
9.	sū per	super	su^{2} per^{3}	L
10.	su per	supper	sup^{3} per^{3}	L
11.	mū vē	movie	mo^{2} vie^{3}	
12.	film	film	film^{4}	
13.	fī nəl	final	fi^{2} nal^{3}	L
14.	fī nəl lē	finally	fi^{2} nal^{3} ly^{2}	
15.	men ē	many	man^{3} y^{1}	
16.				
17.				
18.				
19.				
20.				

ā	âr	är	er	ē	ēr	ī	ō	ŏŏ	ôr	ow	oy	ū	zh	ə
day	air	far	her	bee	tear	light	rope	book	for	cow	boy	tune	vision	item

Day 3

1. ______________ ☐
2. ______________ ☐
3. ______________ ☐
4. ______________ ☐
5. ______________ ☐
6. ______________ ☐
7. ______________ ☐
8. ______________ ☐
9. ______________ ☐
10. ______________ ☐
11. ______________ ☐
12. ______________ ☐
13. ______________ ☐
14. ______________ ☐
15. ______________ ☐
16. ______________ ☐
17. ______________ ☐
18. ______________ ☐
19. ______________ ☐
20. ______________ ☐

Day 4

1. ______________ ☐
2. ______________ ☐
3. ______________ ☐
4. ______________ ☐
5. ______________ ☐
6. ______________ ☐
7. ______________ ☐
8. ______________ ☐
9. ______________ ☐
10. ______________ ☐
11. ______________ ☐
12. ______________ ☐
13. ______________ ☐
14. ______________ ☐
15. ______________ ☐
16. ______________ ☐
17. ______________ ☐
18. ______________ ☐
19. ______________ ☐
20. ______________ ☐

ā	**âr**	**är**	**er**	**ē**	**ēr**	**ī**	**ō**	**ŏŏ**	**ôr**	**ow**	**oy**	**ū**	**zh**	**ə**
day	air	far	her	bee	tear	light	rope	book	for	cow	boy	tune	vision	item

Lesson 17b

1.	sānt pol	Saint Paul	Saint^5 Paul^4
2	Min nə sō də	Minnesota	Min^3 ne^2 so^2 ta^2
3.	jak sən	Jackson	Jack^4 son^3
4.	mis sə sip pē	Mississippi	Mis^3 sis^3 sip^3 pi^2
5.	är tis tik	artistic	ar^2 tis^3 tic^3
6.	thank ful	thankful	thank^5 ful^3
7.	gra di tūd	gratitude	grat^4 i^1 tude^4
8.	klow did	clouded	clou^4 ded^3
9.	sū per	super	su^2 per^3
10.	su per	supper	sup^3 per^3
11.	mū vē	movie	mo^2 vie^3
12.	film	film	film^4
13.	fī nəl	final	fi^2 nal^3
14.	fī nəl lē	finally	fi^2 nal^3 ly^2
15.	men ē	many	man^3 y^1
16.			
17.			
18.			
19.			
20.			

ā	âr	är	er	ē	ēr	ī	ō	ŏŏ	ôr	ow	oy	ū	zh	ə
day	air	far	her	bee	tear	light	rope	book	for	cow	boy	tune	vision	item

Syllable Savvy Spelling Four

Day 1

1. ______________________ ☐
2. ______________________ ☐
3. ______________________ ☐
4. ______________________ ☐
5. ______________________ ☐
6. ______________________ ☐
7. ______________________ ☐
8. ______________________ ☐
9. ______________________ ☐
10. ______________________ ☐
11. ______________________ ☐
12. ______________________ ☐
13. ______________________ ☐
14. ______________________ ☐
15. ______________________ ☐
16. ______________________ ☐
17. ______________________ ☐
18. ______________________ ☐
19. ______________________ ☐
20. ______________________ ☐

Day 2

1. ______________________ ☐
2. ______________________ ☐
3. ______________________ ☐
4. ______________________ ☐
5. ______________________ ☐
6. ______________________ ☐
7. ______________________ ☐
8. ______________________ ☐
9. ______________________ ☐
10. ______________________ ☐
11. ______________________ ☐
12. ______________________ ☐
13. ______________________ ☐
14. ______________________ ☐
15. ______________________ ☐
16. ______________________ ☐
17. ______________________ ☐
18. ______________________ ☐
19. ______________________ ☐
20. ______________________ ☐

ā	âr	är	er	ē	ēr	ī	ō	ŏŏ	ôr	ow	oy	ū	zh	ə
day	air	far	her	bee	tear	light	rope	book	for	cow	boy	tune	vision	item

Lesson 18

1.	jef fer sən si tē	Jefferson City	Jef^{3} fer^{3} son^{3} Ci^{2} ty^{2}	
2.	mi zer ē	Missouri	Mis^{3} sour^{4} i^{1}	
3.	hə lē nə	Helena	He^{2} le^{2} na^{2}	
4.	mon ta nə	Montana	Mon^{3} ta^{2} na^{2}	
5.	tem per	temper	tem^{3} per^{3}	
6.	pâr ents	parents	par^{3} ents^{4}	
7.	kēz	keys	keys^{4}	
8.	kâr ək ter	character	char^{4} act^{3} er^{2}	
9.	fols	false	false^{5}	
10.	res əl	wrestle	wres^{4} tle^{3}	
11.	strīk ēn	striking	strik^{5} ing^{3}	H
12.	lēv	leave	leave^{5}	
13.	lēv ēn	leaving	leav^{4} ing^{3}	H
14.	dē pärt ment	department	de^{2} part^{4} ment^{4}	
15.	kəm pärt ment	compartment	com^{3} part^{4} ment^{4}	
16.				
17.				
18.				
19.				
20.				

ā	âr	är	er	ē	ēr	ī	ō	ŏŏ	ôr	ow	oy	ū	zh	ə
day	air	far	her	bee	tear	light	rope	book	for	cow	boy	tune	vision	item

Day 3

1. ______________________ ☐
2. ______________________ ☐
3. ______________________ ☐
4. ______________________ ☐
5. ______________________ ☐
6. ______________________ ☐
7. ______________________ ☐
8. ______________________ ☐
9. ______________________ ☐
10. ______________________ ☐
11. ______________________ ☐
12. ______________________ ☐
13. ______________________ ☐
14. ______________________ ☐
15. ______________________ ☐
16. ______________________ ☐
17. ______________________ ☐
18. ______________________ ☐
19. ______________________ ☐
20. ______________________ ☐

Day 4

1. ______________________ ☐
2. ______________________ ☐
3. ______________________ ☐
4. ______________________ ☐
5. ______________________ ☐
6. ______________________ ☐
7. ______________________ ☐
8. ______________________ ☐
9. ______________________ ☐
10. ______________________ ☐
11. ______________________ ☐
12. ______________________ ☐
13. ______________________ ☐
14. ______________________ ☐
15. ______________________ ☐
16. ______________________ ☐
17. ______________________ ☐
18. ______________________ ☐
19. ______________________ ☐
20. ______________________ ☐

ā	**âr**	**är**	**er**	**ē**	**ēr**	**ī**	**ō**	**ŏŏ**	**ôr**	**ow**	**oy**	**ū**	**zh**	**ə**
day	air	far	her	bee	tear	light	rope	book	for	cow	boy	tune	vision	item

Lesson 18b

1.	jef fer sən si tē	Jefferson City	Jef^3 fer^3 son^3 Ci^2 ty^2
2.	mi zer ē	Missouri	Mis^3 sour^4 i^1
3.	hə lē nə	Helena	He^2 le^2 na^2
4.	mon ta nə	Montana	Mon^3 ta^2 na^2
5.	tem per	temper	tem^3 per^3
6.	pâr ents	parents	par^3 ents^4
7.	kēz	keys	keys^4
8.	kâr ək ter	character	char^4 act^3 er^2
9.	fols	false	false^5
10.	res əl	wrestle	wres^4 tle^3
11.	strīk ēn	striking	strik^5 ing^3
12.	lēv	leave	leave^5
13.	lēv ēn	leaving	leav^4 ing^3
14.	dē pärt ment	department	de^2 part^4 ment^4
15.	kəm pärt ment	compartment	com^3 part^4 ment^4
16.			
17.			
18.			
19.			
20.			

ā	âr	är	er	ē	ēr	ī	ō	ŏŏ	ôr	ow	oy	ū	zh	ə
day	air	far	her	bee	tear	light	rope	book	for	cow	boy	tune	vision	item

Syllable Savvy Spelling Four

Day 1		Day 2	
1.	☐	1.	☐
2.	☐	2.	☐
3.	☐	3.	☐
4.	☐	4.	☐
5.	☐	5.	☐
6.	☐	6.	☐
7.	☐	7.	☐
8.	☐	8.	☐
9.	☐	9.	☐
10.	☐	10.	☐
11.	☐	11.	☐
12.	☐	12.	☐
13.	☐	13.	☐
14.	☐	14.	☐
15.	☐	15.	☐
16.	☐	16.	☐
17.	☐	17.	☐
18.	☐	18.	☐
19.	☐	19.	☐
20.	☐	20.	☐

ā	âr	är	er	ē	ēr	ī	ō	ŏŏ	ôr	ow	oy	ū	zh	ə
day	air	far	her	bee	tear	light	rope	book	for	cow	boy	tune	vision	item

Lesson 19

1.	lēnk ən	Lincoln	Lin^{3} coln^{4}
2.	nə bra skə	Nebraska	Ne^{2} bra^{3} ska^{3}
3.	kar sən si dē	Carson City	Car^{3} son^{3} Ci^{2} ty^{2}
4.	nə va də	Nevada	Ne^{2} va^{2} da^{2}
5.	wel kəm	welcome	wel^{3} come^{4}
6.	frō zin	frozen	fro^{3} zen^{3}
7.	hī wā	highway	high^{4} way^{3}
8.	krēk (water)	creek	creek^{5}
9.	krēk (sound)	creak	creak^{5}
10.	erth kwāk	earthquake	earth^{5} quake^{5}
11.	kownt	count	count^{5}
12.	rē plī	reply	re^{2} ply^{3}
13.	rē plīz	replies	re^{2} plies^{5}
14.	frus trāt	frustrate	frus^{4} trate^{5}
15.	frus trā shən	frustration	frus^{4} tra^{3} tion^{4}
16.			
17.			
18.			
19.			
20.			

c

ā	âr	är	er	ē	ēr	ī	ō	ŏŏ	ôr	ow	oy	ū	zh	ə
day	air	far	her	bee	tear	light	rope	book	for	cow	boy	tune	vision	item

Day 3		Day 4	
1.	☐	1.	☐
2.	☐	2.	☐
3.	☐	3.	☐
4.	☐	4.	☐
5.	☐	5.	☐
6.	☐	6.	☐
7.	☐	7.	☐
8.	☐	8.	☐
9.	☐	9.	☐
10.	☐	10.	☐
11.	☐	11.	☐
12.	☐	12.	☐
13.	☐	13.	☐
14.	☐	14.	☐
15.	☐	15.	☐
16.	☐	16.	☐
17.	☐	17.	☐
18.	☐	18.	☐
19.	☐	19.	☐
20.	☐	20.	☐

ā	**âr**	**är**	**er**	**ē**	**ēr**	**ī**	**ō**	**ŏŏ**	**ôr**	**ow**	**oy**	**ū**	**zh**	**ə**
day	air	far	her	bee	tear	light	rope	book	for	cow	boy	tune	vision	item

Lesson 19b

1.	lēnk ən	Lincoln	Lin^3 coln^4
2.	nə bra skə	Nebraska	Ne^2 bra^3 ska^3
3.	kar sən si dē	Carson City	Car^3 son^3 Ci^2 ty^2
4.	nə va də	Nevada	Ne^2 va^2 da^2
5.	wel kəm	welcome	wel^3 come^4
6.	frō zin	frozen	fro^3 zen^3
7.	hī wā	highway	high^4 way^3
8.	krēk (water)	creek	creek^5
9.	krēk (sound)	creak	creak^5
10.	erth kwāk	earthquake	earth^5 quake^5
11.	kownt	count	count^5
12.	rē plī	reply	re^2 ply^3
13.	rē plīz	replies	re^2 plies^5
14.	frus trāt	frustrate	frus^4 trate^5
15.	frus trā shən	frustration	frus^4 tra^3 tion^4
16.			
17.			
18.			
19.			
20.			

ā	âr	är	er	ē	ēr	ī	ō	ŏŏ	ôr	ow	oy	ū	zh	ə
day	air	far	her	bee	tear	light	rope	book	for	cow	boy	tune	vision	item

Day 1

1. ______________ ☐
2. ______________ ☐
3. ______________ ☐
4. ______________ ☐
5. ______________ ☐
6. ______________ ☐
7. ______________ ☐
8. ______________ ☐
9. ______________ ☐
10. ______________ ☐
11. ______________ ☐
12. ______________ ☐
13. ______________ ☐
14. ______________ ☐
15. ______________ ☐
16. ______________ ☐
17. ______________ ☐
18. ______________ ☐
19. ______________ ☐
20. ______________ ☐

Day 2

1. ______________ ☐
2. ______________ ☐
3. ______________ ☐
4. ______________ ☐
5. ______________ ☐
6. ______________ ☐
7. ______________ ☐
8. ______________ ☐
9. ______________ ☐
10. ______________ ☐
11. ______________ ☐
12. ______________ ☐
13. ______________ ☐
14. ______________ ☐
15. ______________ ☐
16. ______________ ☐
17. ______________ ☐
18. ______________ ☐
19. ______________ ☐
20. ______________ ☐

ā	**âr**	**är**	**er**	**ē**	**ēr**	**ī**	**ō**	**ŏŏ**	**ôr**	**ow**	**oy**	**ū**	**zh**	**ə**
day	air	far	her	bee	tear	light	rope	book	for	cow	boy	tune	vision	item

Lesson 20

1.	kon kōrd	Concord	Con^{3} cord^{4}
2.	nū hamp sher	New Hampshire	New^{3} Hamp^{4} shire^{5}
3.	tren tən	Trenton	Tren^{4} ton^{3}
4.	nū jer zē	New Jersey	New^{3} Jer^{3} sey^{3}
5.	bu bls	bubbles	bub^{3} bles^{4}
6.	sūt	suit	suit^{4}
7.	frūt	fruit	fruit^{5}
8.	el bō	elbow	el^{2} bow^{3}
9.	kon krēt	concrete	con^{3} crete^{5}
10.	sē ment	cement	ce^{2} ment^{4}
11.	kēz	keys	keys^{4}
12.	picht	pitched	pitch^{5}ed^{2}
13.	dis təns	distance	dis^{3} tance^{5}
14.	kum pâr	compare	com^{3} pare^{4}
15.	fôr ist	forest	for^{3} est^{3}
16.			
17.			
18.			
19.			
20.			

ā	âr	är	er	ē	ēr	ī	ō	o͝o	ôr	ow	oy	ū	zh	ə
day	air	far	her	bee	tear	light	rope	book	for	cow	boy	tune	vision	item

Syllable Savvy Spelling Four

Day 3

1. ______________________ ☐
2. ______________________ ☐
3. ______________________ ☐
4. ______________________ ☐
5. ______________________ ☐
6. ______________________ ☐
7. ______________________ ☐
8. ______________________ ☐
9. ______________________ ☐
10. ______________________ ☐
11. ______________________ ☐
12. ______________________ ☐
13. ______________________ ☐
14. ______________________ ☐
15. ______________________ ☐
16. ______________________ ☐
17. ______________________ ☐
18. ______________________ ☐
19. ______________________ ☐
20. ______________________ ☐

Day 4

1. ______________________ ☐
2. ______________________ ☐
3. ______________________ ☐
4. ______________________ ☐
5. ______________________ ☐
6. ______________________ ☐
7. ______________________ ☐
8. ______________________ ☐
9. ______________________ ☐
10. ______________________ ☐
11. ______________________ ☐
12. ______________________ ☐
13. ______________________ ☐
14. ______________________ ☐
15. ______________________ ☐
16. ______________________ ☐
17. ______________________ ☐
18. ______________________ ☐
19. ______________________ ☐
20. ______________________ ☐

ā	âr	är	er	ē	ēr	ī	ō	ŏŏ	ôr	ow	oy	ū	zh	ə
day	air	far	her	bee	tear	light	rope	book	for	cow	boy	tune	vision	item

Lesson 20b

1.	kon kōrd	Concord	Con^3 cord^4
2.	nū hamp sher	New Hampshire	New^3 Hamp^4 shire^5
3.	tren tən	Trenton	Tren^4 ton^3
4.	nū jer zē	New Jersey	New^3 Jer^3 sey^3
5.	bu bls	bubbles	bub^3 bles^4
6.	sūt	suit	suit^4
7.	frūt	fruit	fruit^5
8.	el bō	elbow	el^2 bow^3
9.	kon krēt	concrete	con^3 crete^5
10.	sē ment	cement	ce^2 ment^4
11.	kēz	keys	keys^4
12.	picht	pitched	pitch^{5}ed^2
13.	dis təns	distance	dis^3 tance^5
14.	kum pâr	compare	com^3 pare^4
15.	fôr ist	forest	for^3 est^3
16.			
17.			
18.			
19.			
20.			

ā	âr	är	er	ē	ēr	ī	ō	ŏŏ	ôr	ow	oy	ū	zh	ə
day	air	far	her	bee	tear	light	rope	book	for	cow	boy	tune	vision	item

Syllable Savvy Spelling Four

Day 1		Day 2	
1.	☐	1.	☐
2.	☐	2.	☐
3.	☐	3.	☐
4.	☐	4.	☐
5.	☐	5.	☐
6.	☐	6.	☐
7.	☐	7.	☐
8.	☐	8.	☐
9.	☐	9.	☐
10.	☐	10.	☐
11.	☐	11.	☐
12.	☐	12.	☐
13.	☐	13.	☐
14.	☐	14.	☐
15.	☐	15.	☐
16.	☐	16.	☐
17.	☐	17.	☐
18.	☐	18.	☐
19.	☐	19.	☐
20.	☐	20.	☐

ā	âr	är	er	ē	ēr	ī	ō	ŏŏ	ôr	ow	oy	ū	zh	ə
day	air	far	her	bee	tear	light	rope	book	for	cow	boy	tune	vision	item

Lesson 21

1.	san tə fā	Santa Fe	San^{3} ta^{2} Fe^{2}
2.	nū mek si kō	New Mexico	New^{3} Mex^{3} i^{1} co^{2}
3.	al bə nē	Albany	Al^{2} ba^{2} ny^{2}
4.	nū yôrk	New York	New^{3} York^{4}
5.	man əj	manage	man^{3} age^{3}
6.	grūp	group	group^{5}
7.	rē əl īz	realize	re^{2} al^{2} ize^{3}
8.	rej ə ster	register	reg^{3} i^{1} ster^{4}
9.	prak ti kl	practical	prac^{4} ti^{2} cal^{3}
10.	sig nəl	signal	sig^{3} nal^{3}
11.	bā sik	basic	ba^{2} sic^{3}
12.	pro blem	problem	prob^{4} lem^{3}
13.	so ker	soccer	soc^{3} cer^{3}
14.	fŏŏt bol	football	foot^{4} ball^{4}
15.	te nis	tennis	ten^{3} nis^{3}
16.			
17.			
18.			
19.			
20.			

ā	âr	är	er	ē	ēr	ī	ō	ŏŏ	ôr	ow	oy	ū	zh	ə
day	air	far	her	bee	tear	light	rope	book	for	cow	boy	tune	vision	item

Day 3		Day 4	
1.	☐	1.	☐
2.	☐	2.	☐
3.	☐	3.	☐
4.	☐	4.	☐
5.	☐	5.	☐
6.	☐	6.	☐
7.	☐	7.	☐
8.	☐	8.	☐
9.	☐	9.	☐
10.	☐	10.	☐
11.	☐	11.	☐
12.	☐	12.	☐
13.	☐	13.	☐
14.	☐	14.	☐
15.	☐	15.	☐
16.	☐	16.	☐
17.	☐	17.	☐
18.	☐	18.	☐
19.	☐	19.	☐
20.	☐	20.	☐

ā	**âr**	**är**	**er**	**ē**	**ēr**	**ī**	**ō**	**o͝o**	**ôr**	**ow**	**oy**	**ū**	**zh**	**ə**
day	air	far	her	bee	tear	light	rope	book	for	cow	boy	tune	vision	item

Lesson 21b

1.	san tə fā	Santa Fe	San^3 ta^2 Fe^2
2.	nū mek si kō	New Mexico	New^3 Mex^3 i^1 co^2
3.	al bə nē	Albany	Al^2 ba^2 ny^2
4.	nū yôrk	New York	New^3 York^4
5.	man əj	manage	man^3 age^3
6.	grūp	group	group^5
7.	rē əl īz	realize	re^2 al^2 ize^3
8.	rej ə ster	register	reg^3 i^1 ster^4
9.	prak ti kl	practical	prac^4 ti^2 cal^3
10.	sig nəl	signal	sig^3 nal^3
11.	bā sik	basic	ba^2 sic^3
12.	pro blem	problem	prob^4 lem^3
13.	so ker	soccer	soc^3 cer^3
14.	fŏŏt bol	football	foot^4 ball^4
15.	te nis	tennis	ten^3 nis^3
16.			
17.			
18.			
19.			
20.			

ā	âr	är	er	ē	ēr	ī	ō	ŏŏ	ôr	ow	oy	ū	zh	ə
day	air	far	her	bee	tear	light	rope	book	for	cow	boy	tune	vision	item

Syllable Savvy Spelling Four

Day 1		Day 2	
1. ______	☐	**1.** ______	☐
2. ______	☐	**2.** ______	☐
3. ______	☐	**3.** ______	☐
4. ______	☐	**4.** ______	☐
5. ______	☐	**5.** ______	☐
6. ______	☐	**6.** ______	☐
7. ______	☐	**7.** ______	☐
8. ______	☐	**8.** ______	☐
9. ______	☐	**9.** ______	☐
10. ______	☐	**10.** ______	☐
11. ______	☐	**11.** ______	☐
12. ______	☐	**12.** ______	☐
13. ______	☐	**13.** ______	☐
14. ______	☐	**14.** ______	☐
15. ______	☐	**15.** ______	☐
16. ______	☐	**16.** ______	☐
17. ______	☐	**17.** ______	☐
18. ______	☐	**18.** ______	☐
19. ______	☐	**19.** ______	☐
20. ______	☐	**20.** ______	☐

ā	**âr**	**är**	**er**	**ē**	**ēr**	**ī**	**ō**	**ŏŏ**	**ôr**	**ow**	**oy**	**ū**	**zh**	**ə**
day	air	far	her	bee	tear	light	rope	book	for	cow	boy	tune	vision	item

Lesson 22

1.	ro lē	Raleigh	Ra^{2} leigh^{5}	S
2.	north kâr ə lī nə	North Carolina	North^{5} Car^{3} o^{1} li^{2} na^{2}	
3.	biz märk	Bismarck	Bis^{3} marck^{5}	
4.	nôrth də kō də	North Dakota	North^{5} Da^{2} ko^{2} ta^{2}	
5.	bās bol	baseball	base^{4} ball^{4}	
6.	swim ēn	swimming	swim^{4} ming^{4}	K
7.	fēld	field	field^{5}	S
8.	hok ē	hockey	hock^{4} ey^{2}	
9.	in ter est*	interest	in^{2} ter^{3} est^{3}	G
10.	in ter est ēn*	interesting	in^{2} ter^{3} est^{3} ing^{3}	
11.	land skāp	landscape	land^{4} scape^{5}	
12.	rē sī kəl	recycle	re^{2} cy^{2} cle^{3}	
13.	ha vēn	having	hav^{3} ing^{3}	H
14.	mō der sī kl	motorcycle	mo^{2} tor^{3} cy^{2} cle^{3}	
15.	ej	edge	edge^{4}	
16.				
17.				
18.				
19.				
20.				

ā	âr	är	er	ē	ēr	ī	ō	ŏŏ	ôr	ow	oy	ū	zh	ə
day	air	far	her	bee	tear	light	rope	book	for	cow	boy	tune	vision	item

Day 3

1. ______________________ ☐
2. ______________________ ☐
3. ______________________ ☐
4. ______________________ ☐
5. ______________________ ☐
6. ______________________ ☐
7. ______________________ ☐
8. ______________________ ☐
9. ______________________ ☐
10. ______________________ ☐
11. ______________________ ☐
12. ______________________ ☐
13. ______________________ ☐
14. ______________________ ☐
15. ______________________ ☐
16. ______________________ ☐
17. ______________________ ☐
18. ______________________ ☐
19. ______________________ ☐
20. ______________________ ☐

Day 4

1. ______________________ ☐
2. ______________________ ☐
3. ______________________ ☐
4. ______________________ ☐
5. ______________________ ☐
6. ______________________ ☐
7. ______________________ ☐
8. ______________________ ☐
9. ______________________ ☐
10. ______________________ ☐
11. ______________________ ☐
12. ______________________ ☐
13. ______________________ ☐
14. ______________________ ☐
15. ______________________ ☐
16. ______________________ ☐
17. ______________________ ☐
18. ______________________ ☐
19. ______________________ ☐
20. ______________________ ☐

ā	**âr**	**är**	**er**	**ē**	**ēr**	**ī**	**ō**	**ŏŏ**	**ôr**	**ow**	**oy**	**ū**	**zh**	**ə**
day	air	far	her	bee	tear	light	rope	book	for	cow	boy	tune	vision	item

Lesson 22b

1.	ro lē	Raleigh	Ra^{2} leigh^{5}
2.	north kâr ə lī nə	North Carolina	North^{5} Car^{3} o^{1} li^{2} na^{2}
3.	biz märk	Bismarck	Bis^{3} marck^{5}
4.	nôrth də kō də	North Dakota	North^{5} Da^{2} ko^{2} ta^{2}
5.	bās bol	baseball	base^{4} ball^{4}
6.	swim ēn	swimming	swim^{4} ming^{4}
7.	fēld	field	field^{5}
8.	hok ē	hockey	hock^{4} ey^{2}
9.	in ter est*	interest	in^{2} ter^{3} est^{3}
10.	in ter est ēn*	interesting	in^{2} ter^{3} est^{3} ing^{3}
11.	land skāp	landscape	land^{4} scape^{5}
12.	rē sī kəl	recycle	re^{2} cy^{2} cle^{3}
13.	ha vēn	having	hav^{3} ing^{3}
14.	mō der sī kl	motorcycle	mo^{2} tor^{3} cy^{2} cle^{3}
15.	ej	edge	edge^{4}
16.			
17.			
18.			
19.			
20.			

ā	âr	är	er	ē	ēr	ī	ō	ŏŏ	ôr	ow	oy	ū	zh	ə
day	air	far	her	bee	tear	light	rope	book	for	cow	boy	tune	vision	item

Syllable Savvy Spelling Four

Day 1		Day 2	
1. ____________	☐	1. ____________	☐
2. ____________	☐	2. ____________	☐
3. ____________	☐	3. ____________	☐
4. ____________	☐	4. ____________	☐
5. ____________	☐	5. ____________	☐
6. ____________	☐	6. ____________	☐
7. ____________	☐	7. ____________	☐
8. ____________	☐	8. ____________	☐
9. ____________	☐	9. ____________	☐
10. ____________	☐	10. ____________	☐
11. ____________	☐	11. ____________	☐
12. ____________	☐	12. ____________	☐
13. ____________	☐	13. ____________	☐
14. ____________	☐	14. ____________	☐
15. ____________	☐	15. ____________	☐
16. ____________	☐	16. ____________	☐
17. ____________	☐	17. ____________	☐
18. ____________	☐	18. ____________	☐
19. ____________	☐	19. ____________	☐
20. ____________	☐	20. ____________	☐

ā	**âr**	**är**	**er**	**ē**	**ēr**	**ī**	**ō**	**ŏŏ**	**ôr**	**ow**	**oy**	**ū**	**zh**	**ə**
day	air	far	her	bee	tear	light	rope	book	for	cow	boy	tune	vision	item

Lesson 23

1.	kə lum bəs	Columbus	Co^{2} lum^{3} bus^{3}
2.	ō hī ō	Ohio	O^{1} hi^{2} o^{1}
3.	ō klə hō mə si dē	Oklahoma City	O^{1} kla^{3} ho^{2} ma^{2} Ci^{2} ty^{2}
4.	ō klə hō mə	Oklahoma	O^{1} kla^{3} ho^{2} ma^{2}
5.	bas kit bol	basketball	bas^{3} ket^{3} ball^{4}
6.	jim nas tiks	gymnastics	gym^{3} nas^{3} tics^{4}
7.	rā sēn	racing	ra^{2} cing^{4}
8.	fôr kast	forecast	fore^{4} cast^{4}
9.	bâr əl	barrel	bar^{3} rel^{3}
10.	ō shn	ocean	o^{1} cean^{4}
11.	bild	build	build^{5}
12.	yôr (belongs to you)	your	your^{4}
13.	yôr (you are)	you're	you^{3} 're^{3}
14.	brī tn	brighten	brigh^{5} ten^{3}
15.	skīz	skies	skies^{5}
16.			
17.			
18.			
19.			
20.			

H

U

N

C

ā	âr	är	er	ē	ēr	ī	ō	ŏŏ	ôr	ow	oy	ū	zh	ə
day	air	far	her	bee	tear	light	rope	book	for	cow	boy	tune	vision	item

Syllable Savvy Spelling Four

Day 3

1. ____________ ☐
2. ____________ ☐
3. ____________ ☐
4. ____________ ☐
5. ____________ ☐
6. ____________ ☐
7. ____________ ☐
8. ____________ ☐
9. ____________ ☐
10. ____________ ☐
11. ____________ ☐
12. ____________ ☐
13. ____________ ☐
14. ____________ ☐
15. ____________ ☐
16. ____________ ☐
17. ____________ ☐
18. ____________ ☐
19. ____________ ☐
20. ____________ ☐

Day 4

1. ____________ ☐
2. ____________ ☐
3. ____________ ☐
4. ____________ ☐
5. ____________ ☐
6. ____________ ☐
7. ____________ ☐
8. ____________ ☐
9. ____________ ☐
10. ____________ ☐
11. ____________ ☐
12. ____________ ☐
13. ____________ ☐
14. ____________ ☐
15. ____________ ☐
16. ____________ ☐
17. ____________ ☐
18. ____________ ☐
19. ____________ ☐
20. ____________ ☐

ā	âr	är	er	ē	ēr	ī	ō	ŏŏ	ôr	ow	oy	ū	zh	ə
day	air	far	her	bee	tear	light	rope	book	for	cow	boy	tune	vision	item

Lesson 23b

1.	kə lum bəs	Columbus	Co^{2} lum^{3} bus^{3}
2.	ō hī ō	Ohio	O^{1} hi^{2} o^{1}
3.	ō klə hō mə si dē	Oklahoma City	O^{1} kla^{3} ho^{2} ma^{2} Ci^{2} ty^{2}
4.	ō klə hō mə	Oklahoma	O^{1} kla^{3} ho^{2} ma^{2}
5.	bas kit bol	basketball	bas^{3} ket^{3} ball^{4}
6.	jim nas tiks	gymnastics	gym^{3} nas^{3} tics^{4}
7.	rā sēn	racing	ra^{2} cing^{4}
8.	fôr kast	forecast	fore^{4} cast^{4}
9.	bâr əl	barrel	bar^{3} rel^{3}
10.	ō shn	ocean	o^{1} cean^{4}
11.	chok	chalk	chalk^{5}
12.	yôr (belongs to you)	your	your^{4}
13.	yôr (you are)	you're	you^{3} 're^{3}
14.	brī tn	brighten	brigh^{5} ten^{3}
15.	skīz	skies	skies^{5}
16.			
17.			
18.			
19.			
20.			

ā	âr	är	er	ē	ēr	ī	ō	ŏŏ	ôr	ow	oy	ū	zh	ə
day	air	far	her	bee	tear	light	rope	book	for	cow	boy	tune	vision	item

Day 1		Day 2	
1.	☐	1.	☐
2.	☐	2.	☐
3.	☐	3.	☐
4.	☐	4.	☐
5.	☐	5.	☐
6.	☐	6.	☐
7.	☐	7.	☐
8.	☐	8.	☐
9.	☐	9.	☐
10.	☐	10.	☐
11.	☐	11.	☐
12.	☐	12.	☐
13.	☐	13.	☐
14.	☐	14.	☐
15.	☐	15.	☐
16.	☐	16.	☐
17.	☐	17.	☐
18.	☐	18.	☐
19.	☐	19.	☐
20.	☐	20.	☐

ā	**âr**	**är**	**er**	**ē**	**ēr**	**ī**	**ō**	**ŏŏ**	**ôr**	**ow**	**oy**	**ū**	**zh**	**ə**
day	air	far	her	bee	tear	light	rope	book	for	cow	boy	tune	vision	item

Lesson 24

1.	sā ləm	Salem	Sa[2] lem[3]
2.	ôr ə gən	Oregon	Or[2] e[1] gon[3]
3.	hâr is berg	Harrisburg	Har[3] ris[3] burg[4]
4.	pen səl vān yə	Pennsylvania	Penn[4] syl[3] van[3] ia[2]
5.	gär bəj	garbage	gar[3] bage[4]
6.	ger oj	garage	gar[3] age[3]
7.	ə kros	across	a[1] cross[5]
8.	skrēn	screen	screen[6]
9.	skrēm	scream	scream[6]
10.	der ekt	direct	dir[3] ect[3]
11.	plād	played	play[4]ed[2]
12.	plad	plaid	plaid[5]
13.	fyū	few	few[3]
14.	ka sl	castle	cas[3] tle[3]
15.	nīts	knights	knights[7]
16.			
17.			
18.			
19.			
20.			

ā	âr	är	er	ē	ēr	ī	ō	ŏŏ	ôr	ow	oy	ū	zh	ə
day	air	far	her	bee	tear	light	rope	book	for	cow	boy	tune	vision	item

Day 3

1. ____________________ ☐
2. ____________________ ☐
3. ____________________ ☐
4. ____________________ ☐
5. ____________________ ☐
6. ____________________ ☐
7. ____________________ ☐
8. ____________________ ☐
9. ____________________ ☐
10. ____________________ ☐
11. ____________________ ☐
12. ____________________ ☐
13. ____________________ ☐
14. ____________________ ☐
15. ____________________ ☐
16. ____________________ ☐
17. ____________________ ☐
18. ____________________ ☐
19. ____________________ ☐
20. ____________________ ☐

Day 4

1. ____________________ ☐
2. ____________________ ☐
3. ____________________ ☐
4. ____________________ ☐
5. ____________________ ☐
6. ____________________ ☐
7. ____________________ ☐
8. ____________________ ☐
9. ____________________ ☐
10. ____________________ ☐
11. ____________________ ☐
12. ____________________ ☐
13. ____________________ ☐
14. ____________________ ☐
15. ____________________ ☐
16. ____________________ ☐
17. ____________________ ☐
18. ____________________ ☐
19. ____________________ ☐
20. ____________________ ☐

ā	**âr**	**är**	**er**	**ē**	**ēr**	**ī**	**ō**	**ŏŏ**	**ôr**	**ow**	**oy**	**ū**	**zh**	**ə**
day	air	far	her	bee	tear	light	rope	book	for	cow	boy	tune	vision	item

Lesson 24b

1.	sā ləm	Salem	Sa[2] lem[3]
2.	ôr ə gən	Oregon	Or[2] e[1] gon[3]
3.	hâr is berg	Harrisburg	Har[3] ris[3] burg[4]
4.	pen səl vān yə	Pennsylvania	Penn[4] syl[3] van[3] ia[2]
5.	gär bəj	garbage	gar[3] bage[4]
6.	ger oj	garage	gar[3] age[3]
7.	ə kros	across	a[1] cross[5]
8.	skrēn	screen	screen[6]
9.	skrēm	scream	scream[6]
10.	der ekt	direct	dir[3] ect[3]
11.	plād	played	play[4]ed[2]
12.	plad	plaid	plaid[5]
13.	fyū	few	few[3]
14.	ka sl	castle	cas[3] tle[3]
15.	nīts	knights	knights[7]
16.			
17.			
18.			
19.			
20.			

ā	âr	är	er	ē	ēr	ī	ō	ŏŏ	ôr	ow	oy	ū	zh	ə
day	air	far	her	bee	tear	light	rope	book	for	cow	boy	tune	vision	item

Day 1

1. ______________ ☐
2. ______________ ☐
3. ______________ ☐
4. ______________ ☐
5. ______________ ☐
6. ______________ ☐
7. ______________ ☐
8. ______________ ☐
9. ______________ ☐
10. ______________ ☐
11. ______________ ☐
12. ______________ ☐
13. ______________ ☐
14. ______________ ☐
15. ______________ ☐
16. ______________ ☐
17. ______________ ☐
18. ______________ ☐
19. ______________ ☐
20. ______________ ☐

Day 2

1. ______________ ☐
2. ______________ ☐
3. ______________ ☐
4. ______________ ☐
5. ______________ ☐
6. ______________ ☐
7. ______________ ☐
8. ______________ ☐
9. ______________ ☐
10. ______________ ☐
11. ______________ ☐
12. ______________ ☐
13. ______________ ☐
14. ______________ ☐
15. ______________ ☐
16. ______________ ☐
17. ______________ ☐
18. ______________ ☐
19. ______________ ☐
20. ______________ ☐

ā	**âr**	**är**	**er**	**ē**	**ēr**	**ī**	**ō**	**ŏŏ**	**ôr**	**ow**	**oy**	**ū**	**zh**	**ə**
day	air	far	her	bee	tear	light	rope	book	for	cow	boy	tune	vision	item

Lesson 25

1.	pro və dent	Provident	Pro^{3} vi^{2} dent^{4}
2.	rōd ī lənd	Rhode Island	Rhode^{5} Is^{2} land^{4}
3.	kə lum bē ə	Columbia	Co^{2} lum^{3} bi^{2} a^{1}
4.	sowth kâr ə lī nə	South Carolina	South^{5} Car^{3} o^{1} li^{2} na^{2}
5.	il ə strāt	illustrate	il^{2} lu^{2} strate^{6}
7.	per sən	person	per^{3} son^{3}
6.	per sən əl	personal	per^{3} son^{3} al^{2}
8.	per sən əl īz	personalize	per^{3} son^{3} al^{2} ize^{3}
9.	sev in	seven	sev^{3} en^{2}
10.	sev in tē	seventy	sev^{3} en^{2} ty^{2}
11.	ā tēn	eighteen	eigh^{4} teen^{4}
12.	ā tē	eighty	eigh^{4} ty^{2}
13.	ē lev in	eleven	e^{1} le^{2} ven^{3}
14.	twelv	twelve	twelve^{6}
15.	fôr dē	forty	for^{3} ty^{2}
16.			
17.			
18.			
19.			
20.			

S

ā	âr	är	er	ē	ēr	ī	ō	ŏŏ	ôr	ow	oy	ū	zh	ə
day	air	far	her	bee	tear	light	rope	book	for	cow	boy	tune	vision	item

Day 3

1. ______ ☐
2. ______ ☐
3. ______ ☐
4. ______ ☐
5. ______ ☐
6. ______ ☐
7. ______ ☐
8. ______ ☐
9. ______ ☐
10. ______ ☐
11. ______ ☐
12. ______ ☐
13. ______ ☐
14. ______ ☐
15. ______ ☐
16. ______ ☐
17. ______ ☐
18. ______ ☐
19. ______ ☐
20. ______ ☐

Day 4

1. ______ ☐
2. ______ ☐
3. ______ ☐
4. ______ ☐
5. ______ ☐
6. ______ ☐
7. ______ ☐
8. ______ ☐
9. ______ ☐
10. ______ ☐
11. ______ ☐
12. ______ ☐
13. ______ ☐
14. ______ ☐
15. ______ ☐
16. ______ ☐
17. ______ ☐
18. ______ ☐
19. ______ ☐
20. ______ ☐

ā	**âr**	**är**	**er**	**ē**	**ēr**	**ī**	**ō**	**ŏŏ**	**ôr**	**ow**	**oy**	**ū**	**zh**	**ə**
day	air	far	her	bee	tear	light	rope	book	for	cow	boy	tune	vision	item

Lesson 25b

1.	pro və dent	Provident	Pro^3 vi^2 dent^4
2.	rōd ī lənd	Rhode Island	Rhode^5 Is^2 land^4
3.	kə lum bē ə	Columbia	Co^2 lum^3 bi^2 a^1
4.	sowth kâr ə lī nə	South Carolina	South^5 Car^3 o^1 li^2 na^2
5.	il ə strāt	illustrate	il^2 lu^2 strate^6
7.	per sən	person	per^3 son^3
6.	per sən əl	personal	per^3 son^3 al^2
8.	per sən əl īz	personalize	per^3 son^3 al^2 ize^3
9.	sev in	seven	sev^3 en^2
10.	sev in tē	seventy	sev^3 en^2 ty^2
11.	ā tēn	eighteen	eigh^4 teen^4
12.	ā tē	eighty	eigh^4 ty^2
13.	ē lev in	eleven	e^1 le^2 ven^3
14.	twelv	twelve	twelve^6
15.	fôr dē	forty	for^3 ty^2
16.			
17.			
18.			
19.			
20.			

ā	âr	är	er	ē	ēr	ī	ō	ŏŏ	ôr	ow	oy	ū	zh	ə
day	air	far	her	bee	tear	light	rope	book	for	cow	boy	tune	vision	item

Syllable Savvy Spelling Four

Day 1

1. ______________________ ☐
2. ______________________ ☐
3. ______________________ ☐
4. ______________________ ☐
5. ______________________ ☐
6. ______________________ ☐
7. ______________________ ☐
8. ______________________ ☐
9. ______________________ ☐
10. ______________________ ☐
11. ______________________ ☐
12. ______________________ ☐
13. ______________________ ☐
14. ______________________ ☐
15. ______________________ ☐
16. ______________________ ☐
17. ______________________ ☐
18. ______________________ ☐
19. ______________________ ☐
20. ______________________ ☐

Day 2

1. ______________________ ☐
2. ______________________ ☐
3. ______________________ ☐
4. ______________________ ☐
5. ______________________ ☐
6. ______________________ ☐
7. ______________________ ☐
8. ______________________ ☐
9. ______________________ ☐
10. ______________________ ☐
11. ______________________ ☐
12. ______________________ ☐
13. ______________________ ☐
14. ______________________ ☐
15. ______________________ ☐
16. ______________________ ☐
17. ______________________ ☐
18. ______________________ ☐
19. ______________________ ☐
20. ______________________ ☐

ā	**âr**	**är**	**er**	**ē**	**ēr**	**ī**	**ō**	**ŏŏ**	**ôr**	**ow**	**oy**	**ū**	**zh**	**ə**
day	air	far	her	bee	tear	light	rope	book	for	cow	boy	tune	vision	item

Lesson 26

1.	pē âr	Pierre	Pi^{2} erre^{4}	
2.	sowth də kō də	South Dakota	South^{5} Da^{2} ko^{2} ta^{2}	
3.	nash vil	Nashville	Nash^{4} ville^{5}	
4.	ten ə sē	Tennessee	Ten^{3} nes^{3} see^{3}	
5.	lärj lē	largely	large^{5} ly^{2}	
6.	wen ev er	whenever	when^{4} ev^{2} er^{2}	
7.	hū ev er	whoever	who^{3} ev^{2} er^{2}	
8.	sum bə dē	somebody	some^{4} bo^{2} dy^{2}	
9.	rē kwest	request	re^{2} quest^{5}	
10.	kwôr ter	quarter	quart^{5} er^{2}	
11.	an ser	answer	an^{2} swer^{4}	D
12.	prin tid	printed	prin^{4} ted^{3}	
13.	klām	claim	claim^{5}	
14.	de zert (sand)	desert	de^{2} sert^{4}	L
15.	dē zert (treat)	dessert	des^{3} sert^{4}	L
16.				
17.				
18.				
19.				
20.				

ā	âr	är	er	ē	ēr	ī	ō	ŏŏ	ôr	ow	oy	ū	zh	ə
day	air	far	her	bee	tear	light	rope	book	for	cow	boy	tune	vision	item

Day 3

1. ____________________ ☐
2. ____________________ ☐
3. ____________________ ☐
4. ____________________ ☐
5. ____________________ ☐
6. ____________________ ☐
7. ____________________ ☐
8. ____________________ ☐
9. ____________________ ☐
10. ____________________ ☐
11. ____________________ ☐
12. ____________________ ☐
13. ____________________ ☐
14. ____________________ ☐
15. ____________________ ☐
16. ____________________ ☐
17. ____________________ ☐
18. ____________________ ☐
19. ____________________ ☐
20. ____________________ ☐

Day 4

1. ____________________ ☐
2. ____________________ ☐
3. ____________________ ☐
4. ____________________ ☐
5. ____________________ ☐
6. ____________________ ☐
7. ____________________ ☐
8. ____________________ ☐
9. ____________________ ☐
10. ____________________ ☐
11. ____________________ ☐
12. ____________________ ☐
13. ____________________ ☐
14. ____________________ ☐
15. ____________________ ☐
16. ____________________ ☐
17. ____________________ ☐
18. ____________________ ☐
19. ____________________ ☐
20. ____________________ ☐

ā	**âr**	**är**	**er**	**ē**	**ēr**	**ī**	**ō**	**ŏŏ**	**ôr**	**ow**	**oy**	**ū**	**zh**	**ə**
day	air	far	her	bee	tear	light	rope	book	for	cow	boy	tune	vision	item

Lesson 26b

1.	pē âr	Pierre	Pi^{2} erre^{4}
2.	sowth də kō də	South Dakota	South^{5} Da^{2} ko^{2} ta^{2}
3.	nash vil	Nashville	Nash^{4} ville^{5}
4.	ten ə sē	Tennessee	Ten^{3} nes^{3} see^{3}
5.	lärj lē	largely	large^{5} ly^{2}
6.	wen ev er	whenever	when^{4} ev^{2} er^{2}
7.	hū ev er	whoever	who^{3} ev^{2} er^{2}
8.	sum bə dē	somebody	some^{4} bo^{2} dy^{2}
9.	rē kwest	request	re^{2} quest^{5}
10.	kwôr ter	quarter	quart^{5} er^{2}
11.	an ser	answer	an^{2} swer^{4}
12.	prin tid	printed	prin^{4} ted^{3}
13.	klām	claim	claim^{5}
14.	de zert (sand)	desert	de^{2} sert^{4}
15.	dē zert (treat)	dessert	des^{3} sert^{4}
16.			
17.			
18.			
19.			
20.			

ā	âr	är	er	ē	ēr	ī	ō	ŏŏ	ôr	ow	oy	ū	zh	ə
day	air	far	her	bee	tear	light	rope	book	for	cow	boy	tune	vision	item

Syllable Savvy Spelling Four

Day 1		Day 2	
1.	☐	1.	☐
2.	☐	2.	☐
3.	☐	3.	☐
4.	☐	4.	☐
5.	☐	5.	☐
6.	☐	6.	☐
7.	☐	7.	☐
8.	☐	8.	☐
9.	☐	9.	☐
10.	☐	10.	☐
11.	☐	11.	☐
12.	☐	12.	☐
13.	☐	13.	☐
14.	☐	14.	☐
15.	☐	15.	☐
16.	☐	16.	☐
17.	☐	17.	☐
18.	☐	18.	☐
19.	☐	19.	☐
20.	☐	20.	☐

ā	âr	är	er	ē	ēr	ī	ō	ŏŏ	ôr	ow	oy	ū	zh	ə
day	air	far	her	bee	tear	light	rope	book	for	cow	boy	tune	vision	item

Lesson 27

1.	os tin	Austin	Aus^{3} tin^{3}	
2.	teks əs	Texas	Tex^{3} as^{2}	
3.	solt lāk si dē	Salt Lake City	Salt^{4} Lake^{4} Ci^{2} ty^{2}	
4.	yū to	Utah	U^{1} tah^{3}	
5.	kun si der	consider	con^{3} si^{2} der^{3}	
6.	rū mer	rumor	ru^{2} mor^{3}	Q
7.	dis kus	discuss	dis^{3} cuss^{4}	
8.	dis ku shn	discussion	dis^{3} cus^{3} sion^{4}	
9.	nokd	knocked	knock^{5}ed^{2}	D
10.	bär rō	borrow	bor^{3} row^{3}	
11.	e ver ē*	every	e^{1} ver^{3} y^{1}	G
12.	plē zēn	pleasing	plea^{4} sing^{4}	H
13.	brāk (crack)	break	break^{5}	
14.	brāk (stop)	brake	brake^{5}	
15.	skwâr	square	square^{6}	
16.				
17.				
18.				
19.				
20.				

ā	âr	är	er	ē	ēr	ī	ō	ŏŏ	ôr	ow	oy	ū	zh	ə
day	air	far	her	bee	tear	light	rope	book	for	cow	boy	tune	vision	item

Syllable Savvy Spelling Four

Day 3

1. ______________ ☐
2. ______________ ☐
3. ______________ ☐
4. ______________ ☐
5. ______________ ☐
6. ______________ ☐
7. ______________ ☐
8. ______________ ☐
9. ______________ ☐
10. ______________ ☐
11. ______________ ☐
12. ______________ ☐
13. ______________ ☐
14. ______________ ☐
15. ______________ ☐
16. ______________ ☐
17. ______________ ☐
18. ______________ ☐
19. ______________ ☐
20. ______________ ☐

Day 4

1. ______________ ☐
2. ______________ ☐
3. ______________ ☐
4. ______________ ☐
5. ______________ ☐
6. ______________ ☐
7. ______________ ☐
8. ______________ ☐
9. ______________ ☐
10. ______________ ☐
11. ______________ ☐
12. ______________ ☐
13. ______________ ☐
14. ______________ ☐
15. ______________ ☐
16. ______________ ☐
17. ______________ ☐
18. ______________ ☐
19. ______________ ☐
20. ______________ ☐

ā	âr	är	er	ē	ēr	ī	ō	ŏŏ	ôr	ow	oy	ū	zh	ə
day	air	far	her	bee	tear	light	rope	book	for	cow	boy	tune	vision	item

Lesson 27b

1.	**os tin**	**Austin**	**Aus^{3} tin^{3}**
2.	**teks əs**	**Texas**	**Tex^{3} as^{2}**
3.	**solt lāk si dē**	**Salt Lake City**	**Salt^{4} Lake^{4} Ci^{2} ty^{2}**
4.	**yū to**	**Utah**	**U^{1} tah^{3}**
5.	**kun si der**	**consider**	**con^{3} si^{2} der^{3}**
6.	**rū mer**	**rumor**	**ru^{2} mor^{3}**
7.	**dis kus**	**discuss**	**dis^{3} cuss^{4}**
8.	**dis ku shn**	**discussion**	**dis^{3} cus^{3} sion^{4}**
9.	**nokd**	**knocked**	**knock^{5}ed^{2}**
10.	**bär rō**	**borrow**	**bor^{3} row^{3}**
11.	**e ver ē***	**every**	**e^{1} ver^{3} y^{1}**
12.	**plē zēn**	**pleasing**	**plea^{4} sing^{4}**
13.	**brāk (crack)**	**break**	**break^{5}**
14.	**brāk (stop)**	**brake**	**brake^{5}**
15.	**skwâr**	**square**	**square^{6}**
16.			
17.			
18.			
19.			
20.			

ā	âr	är	er	ē	ēr	ī	ō	ŏŏ	ôr	ow	oy	ū	zh	ə
day	air	far	her	bee	tear	light	rope	book	for	cow	boy	tune	vision	item

Day 1

1. ______________ ☐
2. ______________ ☐
3. ______________ ☐
4. ______________ ☐
5. ______________ ☐
6. ______________ ☐
7. ______________ ☐
8. ______________ ☐
9. ______________ ☐
10. ______________ ☐
11. ______________ ☐
12. ______________ ☐
13. ______________ ☐
14. ______________ ☐
15. ______________ ☐
16. ______________ ☐
17. ______________ ☐
18. ______________ ☐
19. ______________ ☐
20. ______________ ☐

Day 2

1. ______________ ☐
2. ______________ ☐
3. ______________ ☐
4. ______________ ☐
5. ______________ ☐
6. ______________ ☐
7. ______________ ☐
8. ______________ ☐
9. ______________ ☐
10. ______________ ☐
11. ______________ ☐
12. ______________ ☐
13. ______________ ☐
14. ______________ ☐
15. ______________ ☐
16. ______________ ☐
17. ______________ ☐
18. ______________ ☐
19. ______________ ☐
20. ______________ ☐

ā	**âr**	**är**	**er**	**ē**	**ēr**	**ī**	**ō**	**ŏŏ**	**ôr**	**ow**	**oy**	**ū**	**zh**	**ə**
day	air	far	her	bee	tear	light	rope	book	for	cow	boy	tune	vision	item

Lesson 28

1.	mont pēl yer	Montpelier	Mont^{4} pe^{2} lier^{4}	
2.	ver mont	Vermont	Ver^{3} mont^{4}	
3.	ritch mund	Richmond	Rich^{4} mond^{4}	
4.	ver jin yə	Virginia	Vir^{3} gin^{3} ia^{2}	
5.	târ er	terror	ter^{3} ror^{3}	Q
6.	târ ə bəl	terrible	ter^{3} ri^{2} ble^{3}	
7.	hôr er	horror	hor^{3} ror^{3}	Q
8.	hôr ə bəl	horrible	hor^{3} ri^{2} ble^{3}	
9.	sēng əl	single	sin^{3} gle^{3}	
10.	kli nik	clinic	clin^{4} ic^{2}	
11.	tī erd	tired	tired^{5}	
12.	sī lint	silent	si^{2} lent^{4}	L
13.	ra pid	rapid	rap^{3} id^{2}	L
14.	ə sist	assist	as^{2} sist^{4}	
15.	ə sist əns	assistance	as^{2} sis^{3} tance^{5}	
16.				
17.				
18.				
19.				
20.				

ā	âr	är	er	ē	ēr	ī	ō	ŏŏ	ôr	ow	oy	ū	zh	ə
day	air	far	her	bee	tear	light	rope	book	for	cow	boy	tune	vision	item

Day 3

1. ____________ ☐
2. ____________ ☐
3. ____________ ☐
4. ____________ ☐
5. ____________ ☐
6. ____________ ☐
7. ____________ ☐
8. ____________ ☐
9. ____________ ☐
10. ____________ ☐
11. ____________ ☐
12. ____________ ☐
13. ____________ ☐
14. ____________ ☐
15. ____________ ☐
16. ____________ ☐
17. ____________ ☐
18. ____________ ☐
19. ____________ ☐
20. ____________ ☐

Day 4

1. ____________ ☐
2. ____________ ☐
3. ____________ ☐
4. ____________ ☐
5. ____________ ☐
6. ____________ ☐
7. ____________ ☐
8. ____________ ☐
9. ____________ ☐
10. ____________ ☐
11. ____________ ☐
12. ____________ ☐
13. ____________ ☐
14. ____________ ☐
15. ____________ ☐
16. ____________ ☐
17. ____________ ☐
18. ____________ ☐
19. ____________ ☐
20. ____________ ☐

ā	**âr**	**är**	**er**	**ē**	**ēr**	**ī**	**ō**	**ŏŏ**	**ôr**	**ow**	**oy**	**ū**	**zh**	**ə**
day	air	far	her	bee	tear	light	rope	book	for	cow	boy	tune	vision	item

Lesson 28b

1.	mont pēl yer	Montpelier	Mont^{4} pe^{2} lier^{4}
2.	ver mont	Vermont	Ver^{3} mont^{4}
3.	ritch mund	Richmond	Rich^{4} mond^{4}
4.	ver jin yə	Virginia	Vir^{3} gin^{3} ia^{2}
5.	târ er	terror	ter^{3} ror^{3}
6.	târ ə bəl	terrible	ter^{3} ri^{2} ble^{3}
7.	hôr er	horror	hor^{3} ror^{3}
8.	hôr ə bəl	horrible	hor^{3} ri^{2} ble^{3}
9.	sēng əl	single	sin^{3} gle^{3}
10.	kli nik	clinic	clin^{4} ic^{2}
11.	tī erd	tired	tired^{5}
12.	sī lint	silent	si^{2} lent^{4}
13.	ra pid	rapid	rap^{3} id^{2}
14.	ə sist	assist	as^{2} sist^{4}
15.	ə sist əns	assistance	as^{2} sis^{3} tance^{5}
16.			
17.			
18.			
19.			
20.			

ā	âr	är	er	ē	ēr	ī	ō	ŏŏ	ôr	ow	oy	ū	zh	ə
day	air	far	her	bee	tear	light	rope	book	for	cow	boy	tune	vision	item

Syllable Savvy Spelling Four

Day 1		Day 2	
1.	☐	1.	☐
2.	☐	2.	☐
3.	☐	3.	☐
4.	☐	4.	☐
5.	☐	5.	☐
6.	☐	6.	☐
7.	☐	7.	☐
8.	☐	8.	☐
9.	☐	9.	☐
10.	☐	10.	☐
11.	☐	11.	☐
12.	☐	12.	☐
13.	☐	13.	☐
14.	☐	14.	☐
15.	☐	15.	☐
16.	☐	16.	☐
17.	☐	17.	☐
18.	☐	18.	☐
19.	☐	19.	☐
20.	☐	20.	☐

ā	âr	är	er	ē	ēr	ī	ō	ŏŏ	ôr	ow	oy	ū	zh	ə
day	air	far	her	bee	tear	light	rope	book	for	cow	boy	tune	vision	item

Lesson 29

1.	ə lim pē ə	Olympia	O^{1} lym^{3} pi^{2} a^{1}	
2.	wash ēn tən	Washington	Wash^{4} ing^{3} ton^{3}	
3.	chär əls tən	Charleston	Char^{4} les^{3} ton^{3}	
4.	west ver jin yə	West Virginia	West^{4} Vir^{3} gin^{3} ia^{2}	
5.	poynt	point	point^{5}	
6.	fō dō ko pē	photocopy	pho^{3} to^{2} cop^{3} y^{1}	
7.	huz bənd	husband	hus^{3} band^{4}	
8.	lā dist	latest	la^{2} test^{4}	L
9.	chū ēn	chewing	chew^{4} ing^{3}	
10.	wa gun	wagon	wag^{3} on^{2}	L
11.	tē spūn	teaspoon	tea^{3} spoon^{5}	
12.	tā bl spūn	tablespoon	ta^{2} ble^{3} spoon^{5}	
13.	ka der pil er	caterpillar	cat^{3} er^{2} pil^{3} lar^{3}	R
14.	krē cher	creature	crea^{4} ture^{4}	
15.	chēp	cheap	cheap^{5}	
16.				
17.				
18.				
19.				
20.				

ā	âr	är	er	ē	ēr	ī	ō	o͝o	ôr	ow	oy	ū	zh	ə
day	air	far	her	bee	tear	light	rope	book	for	cow	boy	tune	vision	item

Day 3		Day 4	
1.	☐	1.	☐
2.	☐	2.	☐
3.	☐	3.	☐
4.	☐	4.	☐
5.	☐	5.	☐
6.	☐	6.	☐
7.	☐	7.	☐
8.	☐	8.	☐
9.	☐	9.	☐
10.	☐	10.	☐
11.	☐	11.	☐
12.	☐	12.	☐
13.	☐	13.	☐
14.	☐	14.	☐
15.	☐	15.	☐
16.	☐	16.	☐
17.	☐	17.	☐
18.	☐	18.	☐
19.	☐	19.	☐
20.	☐	20.	☐

ā	âr	är	er	ē	ēr	ī	ō	ŏŏ	ôr	ow	oy	ū	zh	ə
day	air	far	her	bee	tear	light	rope	book	for	cow	boy	tune	vision	item

Lesson 29b

1.	ə lim pē ə	Olympia	O^{1} lym^{3} pi^{2} a^{1}
2.	wash ēn tən	Washington	Wash^{4} ing^{3} ton^{3}
3.	chär əls tən	Charleston	Char^{4} les^{3} ton^{3}
4.	west ver jin yə	West Virginia	West^{4} Vir^{3} gin^{3} ia^{2}
5.	poynt	point	point^{5}
6.	fō dō ko pē	photocopy	pho^{3} to^{2} cop^{3} y^{1}
7.	huz bənd	husband	hus^{3} band^{4}
8.	lā dist	latest	la^{2} test^{4}
9.	chū ēn	chewing	chew^{4} ing^{3}
10.	wa gun	wagon	wa^{2} gon^{3}
11.	tē spūn	teaspoon	tea^{3} spoon^{5}
12.	tā bl spūn	tablespoon	ta^{2} ble^{3} spoon^{5}
13.	ka der pil er	caterpillar	cat^{3} er^{2} pil^{3} lar^{3}
14.	krē cher	creature	crea^{4} ture^{4}
15.	chēp	cheap	cheap^{5}
16.			
17.			
18.			
19.			
20.			

ā	âr	är	er	ē	ēr	ī	ō	ŏŏ	ôr	ow	oy	ū	zh	ə
day	air	far	her	bee	tear	light	rope	book	for	cow	boy	tune	vision	item

Day 1

1. ______________________ ☐

2. ______________________ ☐

3. ______________________ ☐

4. ______________________ ☐

5. ______________________ ☐

6. ______________________ ☐

7. ______________________ ☐

8. ______________________ ☐

9. ______________________ ☐

10. ______________________ ☐

11. ______________________ ☐

12. ______________________ ☐

13. ______________________ ☐

14. ______________________ ☐

15. ______________________ ☐

16. ______________________ ☐

17. ______________________ ☐

18. ______________________ ☐

19. ______________________ ☐

20. ______________________ ☐

Day 2

1. ______________________ ☐

2. ______________________ ☐

3. ______________________ ☐

4. ______________________ ☐

5. ______________________ ☐

6. ______________________ ☐

7. ______________________ ☐

8. ______________________ ☐

9. ______________________ ☐

10. ______________________ ☐

11. ______________________ ☐

12. ______________________ ☐

13. ______________________ ☐

14. ______________________ ☐

15. ______________________ ☐

16. ______________________ ☐

17. ______________________ ☐

18. ______________________ ☐

19. ______________________ ☐

20. ______________________ ☐

ā	**âr**	**är**	**er**	**ē**	**ēr**	**ī**	**ō**	**ŏŏ**	**ôr**	**ow**	**oy**	**ū**	**zh**	**ə**
day	air	far	her	bee	tear	light	rope	book	for	cow	boy	tune	vision	item

Lesson 30

1.	mad ə sən	Madison	Mad^{3} i^{1} son^{3}	
2.	wiz kon sən	Wisconsin	Wis^{3} con^{3} sin^{3}	
3.	shī an	Cheyenne	Chey^{4} enne^{4}	
4.	wī ō mēn	Wyoming	Wy^{2} o^{1} ming^{4}	
5.	pers	purse	purse^{5}	
6.	ī dē əz	ideas	i^{1} de^{2} as^{2}	
7.	kwīt	quite	quite^{5}	
8.	kwī it	quiet	qui^{3} et^{2}	
9.	sprād	sprayed	spray^{5}ed^{2}	J
10.	kon takt	contact	con^{3} tact^{4}	
11.	bŏŏ cher	butcher	but^{3} cher^{4}	
12.	tosd	tossed	toss^{4}ed^{2}	J
13.	pri zə ner	prisoner	pri^{3} son^{3} er^{2}	
14.	fē cher	feature	fea^{3} ture^{4}	
15.	vā kā shn	vacation	va^{2} ca^{2} tion^{4}	L
16.				
17.				
18.				
19.				
20.				

ā	âr	är	er	ē	ēr	ī	ō	ŏŏ	ôr	ow	oy	ū	zh	ə
day	air	far	her	bee	tear	light	rope	book	for	cow	boy	tune	vision	item

Day 3

1. ______________________ ☐
2. ______________________ ☐
3. ______________________ ☐
4. ______________________ ☐
5. ______________________ ☐
6. ______________________ ☐
7. ______________________ ☐
8. ______________________ ☐
9. ______________________ ☐
10. ______________________ ☐
11. ______________________ ☐
12. ______________________ ☐
13. ______________________ ☐
14. ______________________ ☐
15. ______________________ ☐
16. ______________________ ☐
17. ______________________ ☐
18. ______________________ ☐
19. ______________________ ☐
20. ______________________ ☐

Day 4

1. ______________________ ☐
2. ______________________ ☐
3. ______________________ ☐
4. ______________________ ☐
5. ______________________ ☐
6. ______________________ ☐
7. ______________________ ☐
8. ______________________ ☐
9. ______________________ ☐
10. ______________________ ☐
11. ______________________ ☐
12. ______________________ ☐
13. ______________________ ☐
14. ______________________ ☐
15. ______________________ ☐
16. ______________________ ☐
17. ______________________ ☐
18. ______________________ ☐
19. ______________________ ☐
20. ______________________ ☐

ā	**âr**	**är**	**er**	**ē**	**ēr**	**ī**	**ō**	**ŏŏ**	**ôr**	**ow**	**oy**	**ū**	**zh**	**ə**
day	air	far	her	bee	tear	light	rope	book	for	cow	boy	tune	vision	item

Lesson 30b

1.	mad ə sən	Madison	Mad^{3} i^{1} son^{3}
2.	wiz kon sən	Wisconsin	Wis^{3} con^{3} sin^{3}
3.	shī an	Cheyenne	Chey^{4} enne^{4}
4.	wī ō mēn	Wyoming	Wy^{2} o^{1} ming^{4}
5.	pers	purse	purse^{5}
6.	ī dē əz	ideas	i^{1} de^{2} as^{2}
7.	kwīt	quite	quite^{5}
8.	kwī it	quiet	qui^{3} et^{2}
9.	sprād	sprayed	spray^{5}ed^{2}
10.	kon takt	contact	con^{3} tact^{4}
11.	bŏŏ cher	butcher	but^{3} cher^{4}
12.	tosd	tossed	toss^{4}ed^{2}
13.	pri zə ner	prisoner	pri^{3} son^{3} er^{2}
14.	fē cher	feature	fea^{3} ture^{4}
15.	vā kā shn	vacation	va^{2} ca^{2} tion^{4}
16.			
17.			
18.			
19.			
20.			

ā	âr	är	er	ē	ēr	ī	ō	ŏŏ	ôr	ow	oy	ū	zh	ə
day	air	far	her	bee	tear	light	rope	book	for	cow	boy	tune	vision	item

Spelling Rules

A

Short and Long Vowels

Unless otherwise stated, use the short vowel sound in a word.

sad bed lid box sun

A long vowel sound is indicated with a line over the top of the vowel.

ā ē ī ō ū

day bee light rope tune

B

The Schwa

ə

This symbol designates an unstressed "uh" sound. Instead of a schwa, a short u is used if the syllable is stressed.

hum **bəg** **humbug** **hum^{3} bug^{3}**

Both have the same sound, but the short u is stressed and the schwa is unstressed.

C

Y to I Rule

When adding "s" to a word that ends in "y" to make it plural, change the **y** to **i** and add **es**

study studies

D

Silent Letters

Sometimes there is a silent letter in a word that does not make a sound. The pronunciation changed over the years but the spelling did not.

talk

E

F to V

A word that ends in F or FE will be changed to VES to make it plural.

knife knives

Add ES

Add **ES** instead of **S** to make the plural of words ending in S, SH, or CH.

glass glasses

G

Very Different Pronunciations

The spelling and pronunciation of some words are very different. Sometimes the number of syllables is even different. It often helps to remember a unique pronunciation for these unusual words.

February	**feb RU âr ē**
average	**av ER əj**
leopard	**le O pard**
interest	**in TER est**
every	**ē VER ē**

H

ING after Silent E

Drop the **E** at the end of a word when adding **ING**.

bike **biking**

I

ED after Silent E

Drop the **E** at the end of a word when adding **ED or ER.**

bike **biked** **biker**

J

ED

The past tense of most words is formed by adding ED to the end. The word may be pronounced "ed" or "d" or "t" at the end.

"d" **used**

"ed" **headed**

"t" **clapped**

Note that some of these words are pronounced as a single syllable. We have removed the space in the third column to show one syllable.

clapt **clapped** **clap^{4}ped^3**

Double Consonant

Double the consonant when adding an ending with these 3 conditions

1. Word ends with a single consonant (*hop; not hope or hurt*)
2. The letter before the consonant is a single vowel (*hop; not meat*)
3. The ending begins with a vowel (*ed or ing; not hops*)

hopping **hopped**

L

Open and Closed Syllables

A syllable with a short vowel sound is usually closed by a consonant at the end. A syllable with a long vowel sound is usually open with the vowel at the end of the syllable.

tā bl	**table**	**ta^2 ble^3**
ta blit	**tablet**	**tab^3 let^3**

In the word "tablet," the "b" is usually pronounced with the second syllable and not the first. However, since the "a" is a short vowel sound, it is closed with the "b" at the end of the syllable. This rule will assist in learning the spellings of many larger words.

"I" makes Long "E" Sound

Some words from other countries have an "I" that says "E."

radio

N

IGH

Long I sound

high **light** **bright**

O

OUGH

Can make the sound of **o** or **ō** or **ū**

thought **though** **through**

P

AUGH

Can make the sound of **o** or **a**

taught **caught** **haughty** **naughty**

laugh

Q

OR

Some careers end in **OR** instead of ER.

doctor **sailor** **pastor**

Draw a picture: *"Rub-A-Dub-Dub some men in a tub and their name ends in OR"*

R

AR

There are a limited number of words with "ar" at the end with the "er" sound.

sugar **dollar** **pillar**

S

I before E *"believe"*

Except After "C" *"receive"*

Or with a long "A" as in "*neighbor*" or "*weigh*."

T

Different Endings - Same Sound

tion **sion** **cian**

tial **cial**

ous **ious** **eous**

U

Contractions

An apostrophe takes the place of a missing letter or letters.

didn't **they'll** **he's** **I've**